WIDENING
PARTICIPATION
Which way forward
for English higher
education?

Edited by Chris Duke and
Geoff Layer

promoting adult learning

Action on Access
Widening Participation
in Higher Education

D0316850

Published by the National Institute of Adult Continuing Education (England and Wales)
21 De Montfort Street
Leicester LE1 7GE

Company registration no. 2603322
Charity registration no. 1002775

NIACE works to develop increased participation in education and training, particularly for those who do not have easy access because of barriers of class, gender, age, race, language and culture, learning difficulties and disabilities, or insufficient financial resources.

NIACE's website on the Internet is **www.niace.org.uk**

Cataloguing in Publication Data
A CIP record of this title is available from the British Library

ISBN 1 86201 271 7
Typeset by Book Production Services, London

Contents

Introduction
Geoff Layer and Chris Duke

This book grew from a number of conversations about the nature and purpose of access to and widening participation (W/P) within higher education (HE) in England. It is also itself a part of those conversations. Changes are intended to widen participation and make the system more inclusive. Many government departments, funding councils, planning agencies and providers are committed to securing a more inclusive higher education system; the Government has a target for 50 per cent of 18–30 year olds benefiting from higher education by 2010. Alongside this target, ambitious by English if not by OECD standards, is a deep desire to broaden participation. This is to be welcomed, given the imbalance that sees the middle and professional classes dominating higher education.

Approaching the end of 2005, we are at half-time on the journey to 2010. It is opportune to reflect on the journey so far, asking what we now mean by widening participation, how different types of institutions respond to the agenda, and whether interpretations are broad enough. This was the challenge posed to a number of commentators, managers, researchers and providers brought together at NIACE in July 2005 to present short papers for debate and discussion. Most of these have been developed as the substance of this book, with the addition of one further paper. The chapters are as the contributors wished them to be, reflecting their particular perspectives. The focus of the July colloquium was on developing a shared understanding of the diversity of approaches to widening participation to HE, and the working of partnership delivery.

The aim of the book is to take forward the issues, stimulating further discussion, clearer understanding and better action. Many argue that the current policy drive is overly focused on young people and initial higher education. Acknowledging that dilemma, this book concentrates on this youthful aspect of the policy agenda, reflecting on progress towards the target. It does not do this by looking at participation rate changes, but rather in a quest for broad understanding of the sector, and awareness of what needs clarifying in order to achieve a quantum shift.

The colloquium was planned to draw contributors from a range of relevant backgrounds and perspectives. Whilst the majority were from the higher education sector, we also have reflections from such other areas as schools, further education, and the National Health Service. Too often, contributors to such analysis are only from an HE sector introspectively reflecting upon itself.

The chapters that follow are organised thematically, but consistent messages come through. This introduction pulls together some threads and implications.

The commencing overview briefly traces the history of the HE sector in widening participation. It looks at different aspects of participation addressed by universities and colleges. As in the book as a whole, the focus is predominantly on young people. The overview highlights policy tensions that exist, recognising that although some policies have competing implications, universities and colleges are used to operating in just such an environment.

There follow three chapters reflect on issues and progress from the perspectives of contributors managing very different types of institutions. Willcocks provides an insight from the perspective of higher education Colleges, a group of providers originating from diverse backgrounds and established for specific reasons. Today they provide a broad higher education experience. Willcocks shows the contributions that they have made to broadening participation and providing educational opportunities. This is followed by Stuart's reflections from a research-intensive university. She identifies issues that their focus on research excellence raises today, but also notes the challenge that many research-intensive universities originally faced: the introduction of vocational degrees such as engineering. Indeed it is noticeable that both Willcocks and Stuart, from different perspectives, reject simplistic measures to distinguish between HE providers, instead calling for evaluations to be based on *fitness for purpose*. This challenges part of the policy rhetoric masquerading under the expression *fair access*, a policy objective whereby the government would like to see more students from low-income groups enter 'elite' universities. Such students will enter HE anyway; the policy is really about which university or course they go to. Willcocks refers to a 'boarding school culture'; Stuart to a pecking order. Both argue that each learner needs to find the right place for their own purposes within a diverse sector, adopting in other words a learner-centred perspective rather than one driven by traditional assumptions about what is best.

Widdowson explores the role of larger HE providers within the further education (FE) sector, as well as looking from FE generally. Again, there is reference to stratification amongst HE providers, and to students needing a full understanding of the HE curriculum on offer in order to make an informed choice of what and where to study. Widdowson argues passionately that the college sector provide accessibility and opportunities for students who would not otherwise engage in HE. The colleges operate in a very complex part of the tertiary sector, and have to be responsive to new routes, programmes and markets before they are fully embedded as part of HE. This is far removed from the limited scope of *fair access*, but is vital to achieving the policy objectives of expansion and the Skills Strategy.

The book then moves to another theme: different models and markets for higher education. Widdowson started that discussion, and in chapters 5 and 6 Longhurst and Fryer develop it further. Longhurst from his unique position assesses the role of Foundation Degrees in widening participation. He builds on Widdowson's provider perspective to explore the concept behind Foundation Degrees, and their role in stimulating curriculum change and providing programmes based on employer needs. The focus on those already in employment means that the main age group is older than in the Government target. It also leads to courses not based on progression direct from full-time 14–19 provision. This is, however, an important group, as Fryer demonstrates in looking at different forms of learning, recognising more informal and less traditional patterns. Fryer explores the employee development concept that informed activity within the NHS, especially the hard-to-reach outside traditional educational structures. It is easier to get a message about higher education to someone in a traditional classroom setting than it is to workers on the hospital ward or shop floor.

The next theme is the chances that young people may have to move into higher education. This can depend on where they live and what they know about the system. Sheedy argues that life chances vary based on class, geography and culture. He talks about the societal differences that the school structure has to deal with, and argues powerfully that higher education needs to change to meet the needs of learners. Nursaw then explains the ideas behind the development of Compact Schemes designed to support learners from disadvantaged communities who have the potential to succeed. Here is an interesting example of how initiatives develop locally in different ways, but then need to be addressed through a set of principles and in practice. Both Sheedy and Nursaw come back to the issue of guidance, and of individuals being able to make an informed choice.

There follow two chapters that look at higher education internally. Thomas takes learning and teaching in HE, starting from the premise that widening participation needs to be addressed holistically by institutions. It is about not only who takes part, but also student success and achievement. This leads in to Allen focusing on the implications for staff in higher education. Both argue the need for change based on learner need, staff development and the sharing of good practice.

Writing in a personal capacity, Whitston then reflects on consequences determined by the structure of society. Based on research evidence that demonstrates the impact of inequality, he asserts that in essence social class is the greatest single determinant of individual success or failure. He goes on to suggest how HE providers could engage to make HE more inclusive.

The final section offers perspectives by Duke and Watson that reflect on the issues of participation, success and institutional change. Duke looks back over messages provided by the contributors, whereas Watson focuses on the nature of participation.

As the book developed it was interesting to see distinctions between planners, looking for a stratification of higher education, and managers rejecting this as simplistic. The argument for learner-centred diversification based on fitness for purpose is powerful. Such an argument rejects stratification, instead favouring the needs of students to take the appropriate course.

There is a clear message that working in partnership is important, and that current levels and breadth of advice and guidance are inadequate. This is crucially important as the government adopts greater consumer choice. Choice really only exists if you know about it, are aware of the consequences, and can actually decide what to do. Otherwise choice is available only to the 'haves' in society; the 'have-nots' are left to fit in where and as best they can.

A general message from all contributors is of the danger that current initiatives could be missing the main mark. Whitston begins to address this in his section on how HEFCE may be working more closely with HE providers to develop more strategic approaches.

In order to secure a more inclusive higher education, these contributions argue, institutions are complex bodies, stratification is the issue for planners rather than learners, and there must be a broad perspective for widening participation. Rather than focus on young people from lower socio-economic groups entering 'elite' universities, the need is to enhance progression and opportunities on a much broader basis. To increase and broaden participation we need more guidance provision to ensure that potential learners know what is available. Here, potential learners are not just those in full-time education, but also those in the workplace. Similarly there is a need to reflect on the changing composition of the student body, and to make sure that the curriculum and support structures are appropriate to student needs.

Alongside the emphasis on guidance, and a curriculum response within higher education, there is also the thrust of the change necessary to address vocational routes into degrees and diplomas. Key to this debate is whether we see higher education as a system based on three-year full-time degrees for students direct from A-levels; or whether the system accepts the change that is needed. This means a sector planning new routes, recognising adults as part of the target group, securing the engagement of employees through earning while learning, using part-time study, and modernising the learning experience.

These are big challenges for the sector. If we are to be inclusive we need to recognise different forms of participation, and not be caught up in models of the past.

1

Widening participation – an overview

Geoff Layer

The election of a Labour government in 1997 has led to a welcome, clear and consistent drive towards greater inclusivity and success in education. As always, there are many different views amongst individuals, sectoral groups and institutions concerning the focus and usefulness of government intervention.

Many commentators argue that since 1997 all Labour has done is to introduce a series of semi-connected initiatives without any overall strategic focus, and merely placed an intolerable burden of constant change on the delivery agents – schools, colleges and universities. Others will argue that it has embedded accountability and performance measurement into the education system, requiring increased participation and attainment.

What is clear, though, is that the government has approached policy in higher education differentially to other sectors. The agenda in schools and colleges has been dominated by the drive to raise standards and levels of achievement. This is seen in the White Paper on 14–19 (DfES, 2005b), the Skills White Paper (DfES, 2005a) and in a multitude of government initiatives. However, the agenda in higher education is not focused on attainment but on who participates (DfES, 2003b and c). The internal structures of the organisations supporting the management of the system replicate this: the DfES Directorate of Lifelong Learning has a large team known as the 'Standards Unit', whereas the Higher Education Funding Council for England (HEFCE) has a Widening Participation team. That is not to say that universities are not seeking to raise attainment levels, or that schools and colleges are not seeking to be more inclusive; it is simply recognising a policy distinction between sectors.

This paper seeks to explore the background to widening participation in higher education, and consider the policy context and briefly the role of higher education providers.

The key issues that have to be addressed following the analysis of the current position are the matters that have to be achieved to begin to make a real difference. This means that the sector needs to address the major question of what the role of HE actually is. Is it to provide access to an 'academic finishing school' model for students who have been prepared for this traditional experience? Or is it to provide opportunities for a broader range of individuals to study for higher-level awards and to gain the social and economic benefits of a degree? One model is very much focused on students fitting in to an existing model of HE, the other is about the extent to which HE needs to change.

Whilst there is an overt policy commitment to widening participation there is considerable debate about what this actually means. As is always the case when reflecting on the evolution of educational systems, there is a contested history of how we got to where we are and why. Rarely does such a reflection look back at major policy objectives or plans and find it possible to say 'this was the rationale and there was a coherent plan to achieve it'. It is much more common to find that there have been a number and range of conflicting and interlinked policies and plans that have led to the development of the sector in this way. The history of widening participation is no different to most of the change within HE, although today a very narrow perspective has been developed to reflect current policy issues.

A short history could begin with the influence of the universities that now largely comprise the Russell Group in seeking to offer opportunities to adults to study on a part-time basis. This activity was developed through extramural departments and focused on the use of outreach centres to provide different opportunities. This was at a time when very few people went to university and they were almost exclusively young people. This was an era when adult education was a radical initiative designed to develop a civil and just society, territory later claimed by David Blunkett in *The Learning Age* (DfEE, 1998). The universities were allocated geographical areas in which they organised such provision and became known as 'Responsible Bodies'. As HE developed, the roles these bodies performed became more marginalised within the university as the focus became more about 'mainstream' students and research. There is little evidence that once HE became more universally available these forms of provision actually widened participation as opposed to providing adult education at a subsidised rate to the middle classes. It is notable that many of the universities involved have recently reviewed this type of provision and in many cases withdrawn or changed the focus of the service.

The establishment of the polytechnics in 1967 brought a new perspective to HE, with the introduction of a more vocational approach to the targeting of mature students and the inclusion of part-time study. Unlike the Responsible Body approach outlined above, the polytechnics included part-time study, generally vocational in nature, as part of their mainstream provision. The polytechnics provided other routes and awards than full degrees, through HND/Cs and the Diploma of Higher Education, tending to serve their local community and provide more flexible programmes. The funded expansion of the late 1980s and early 90s saw a shift in emphasis, as they were encouraged to increase full-time degree numbers because of the funding methodology. The subsequent award of the 'university' title, the granting of degree-awarding powers and the shift to a combined funding council without planning powers effectively created a sector that encouraged some individual new universities to 'ape' the existing universities. It is notable that at a time when supply and demand for places are effectively balanced the student profile of some former polytechnics is similar to traditional universities', reflecting the success that some have had with that strategy. Indeed, one former polytechnic now has an intake from state schools lower than the 80 per cent cutoff point (HEFCE, HESA Performance Indicators 2001–2004).

This was followed by a stage in which there was a general development of target groups and a recognition that new or alternative entry routes were required. The then Department for Education and Science (DES) recognised that there was a problem in the recruitment of teachers from what are now known as minority ethnic groups. All too often there were no role models of black or Asian teachers to inspire young people. It was believed that older members of these communities generally wanted to help young people but did not have the entry qualifications to become teachers or social workers. The DES therefore worked with a number of LEAs to develop an alternative route into teacher training for adult students. This was the birth of the Access Course. These courses tended to be delivered in FE colleges with a curriculum designed in conjunction with a HEI so that progression could take place. An example of this type of arrangement can be found in Sheffield College.

In 1985 Sheffield City Council identified that they had a growing Afro-Caribbean community but very few teachers, social workers and managers from that background who could provide community understanding and links. They were very conscious that they had a white professional workforce, that their black employees fulfilled manual roles, and that this model tended to be self-replicating. The student recruitment pattern in local HEIs was unlikely to make any real difference given the preponderance of whites in the intake. Therefore the council decided to try to redress the problem through developing a Black Access Course in Sheffield College, which developed progression routes from the Access Course to degrees in Housing, Public Administration, Teacher Training and Social Work, all of which led to appropriate employment with the Council.

The scheme was successful in raising the issue, proposing a solution, and developing a culture within the communities that they could gain such employment. This enabled some students to move into key jobs and then to act as role models for the next generation.

The Access movement was one of the most influential factors in curriculum change within HEIs as it required the matching of the needs of the discipline with that of the learner. In the early days of this initiative the focus was on developing an Access Course to fit the degree course. As they developed, the partners became more skilled in identifying a match between the outcomes of the degree and the Access year so that the learner had more likelihood of success. This was a period of real challenge, innovation and creativity (Layer, 2004) but is crucial to the real question 'Access to What?' (McCormick, 2005; Stuart, 2005), which raises the issue that it is all very well changing participation but is the curriculum ready? All too often there were claims that the Access Course inspired the student but they felt unsupported in the university. The transition to being an independent learner was often not as rapid as the HEI wanted or required, which is a lesson for all types of student progression links and is about the curriculum and the transition needed to reflect the starting point of the learner.

The links between colleges, polytechnics and universities around the Access Course led to much of the expansion of HE in FE through a franchise model in the late 1980s and early 90s. This form of partnership was intended to provide local opportunities for students to study in higher education and represented a major unplanned expansion (Parry, 2005) but which was more regulated in Scotland (Field, 2005). Most of the relationships were bilateral between a HEI and a FEC and have laid much of the foundations of the putative Lifelong Learning Networks (Newby, 2004).

The focus through the 1980s and 1990s was very much on women returners, women in non-traditional subjects and minority ethnic groups. This focus came from champions in institutions, pressure groups, community activists and in some instances corporate strategies. There was no overall political strategy from government other than tacit recommendations that under-represented groups should be better represented. A very different picture to Australia, which developed a policy through Fair Chance for All (DEET, 1990) that universities needed Equity Plans that focused on:

- Aborigines and Torres Strait Islanders;
- disabled students;
- women in non-traditional subjects;

- people from non-English-speaking backgrounds;
- people from low-income groups;
- rural, isolated groups.

This Australian framework represented a national strategy to address particular issues. Such a national strategy was missing when Labour came into power in 1997 and in many respects is still missing. Labour has introduced a focus but it is one riddled with contradictions and lacking clarity or definition.

The shift introduced by New Labour was to focus on young working-class participation.

Vocational routes	Standards
• Foundation Degrees • Skills agenda	• Gold standard routes • Preservation of elite

Figure 1. Policy contradictions

Figure 1 demonstrates the major contradiction in government policy. It firmly believes that in order to produce the workforce necessary for the global economy there is an urgent requirement for more vocational qualifications and routes. On the other hand it is fully committed to maintaining academic standards by the preservation of the 'gold standards' of A-levels and three-year honours degrees in the most 'prestigious' universities. To date it has tried but failed to marry these two principles, and each has different champions. The 'vocational' case is driven very much by a human capital approach, whereas much of the agenda around inclusivity for low-income groups within the 'standards' route is contained in the social capital approach (Schuller, 1997; Coffield 1999; Field, 2005).

Figure 2 demonstrates the stark fact that if a young person comes from a relatively prosperous family then they are much more likely to enter HE. The concept of 'money providing greater individual opportunity' was quite rightly anathema to the Labour government. This is a major challenge and one that the sector has been overdue in addressing.

Figure 3 shows the recruitment of students from the lower socio-economic groups into HE over the period 1960–2000. The data demonstrate that although the numbers from low-income groups did increase significantly over that period, to the proportion entering from the middle and professional classes increased at a faster rate. The year 2000 was the start of a number of initiatives focusing on increasing participation from those groups. The data up to 2000 were used by the DfES in their consultation on the establishment of OFFA, following the White Paper *The*

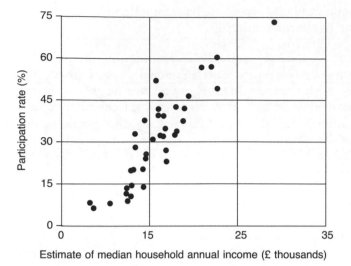

Figure 2: Comparison of participation rates and family income
(Source: HEFCE, 2001c).

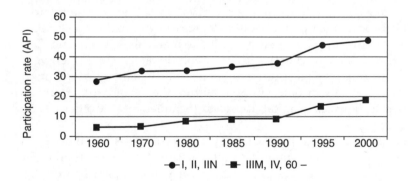

Figure 3: Participation by social class of students in full-time higher education
(Source: DfES, 2003a)

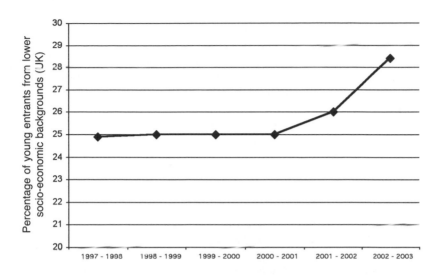

Figure 4: Percentage of young entrants from lower socio-economic
backgrounds

(Source: HEFCE/HESA Performance Indicator Tables, 1996–2003)

Future of Higher Education (DfES, 2003b), in the subsequent Higher
Education Act 2004.

If the DfES had been able to take into account the progress between
2000 and 2002 they would have seen the start of a change in the participation levels, as is shown in Figure 4, although the data are marginally
skewed because of a definitional change.

The policy drive that flows from these data has in a number of
instances been disconnected in a way that inhibits the real progress that
could be made.

A quick summary of the key issues would be:

• As 90 per cent of young people with two A-levels already enter
  HE, will we see real change by focusing on that traditional route?
• If the real issue regarding participation in HE is performance and
  motivation at the age of 16, why has the government sought to
  regulate HE providers to achieve wider participation?
• The absence of any proposals concerning part-time routes in to HE
  is in direct contrast to the focus of the skills White Papers (DfES,
  2003a, 2005) which concentrate on raising skill levels within the
  workforce.
• The inability to ensure that vocational progression to and through
  HE is embedded within and across the system leads many to question the value of the route.

- To date the failure to get the message across that the changing student financial support position means that we are partially returning to the pre-1997 position of HE being free at the point of entry hits the widening participation agenda.
- The continued failure of policy makers to decide whether they want simply to redistribute working-class students around the system or actually broaden participation. The former implies a focus on a small minority of the youth cohort in any one year and will not widen participation in the sector but only succeed in 'moving the deckchairs around'.
- The constant focus on full-time honours degrees as being the dominant form of HE simply means that other routes stagnate or are perceived as second class.
- The lack of any real joined-up thinking between the allocation of Widening Participation Premium and the absence of fairness in the bursaries provisions in the Higher Education Act 2004 reflects the absence of thought-through policy.
- The notion that the Schwartz (2004) review of admissions policies and practices which focuses on narrow perspectives of HE, will help achieve greater inclusivity when it primarily looks at processes for those already likely to enter HE.

So where does this leave the HE sector? It is possible to raise more questions about the impact of participation and the gaps in the analysis that have led to policy development. Of course individual HEIs will have very different reasons for their strategies and approaches to widening participation. In 1999 HEIs were required (HEFCE, 2000) to produce initial statements on widening participation. These statements were opportunities for universities and colleges to articulate what they were doing and why. The guidance given to HEIs was permissive and allowed for a variety of responses. In their analysis of these initial statements Action on Access (2000) found:

> *In 1999 the guidance provided to universities and colleges was very broad and non-prescriptive. The analysis that was undertaken highlighted areas of both strengths and weaknesses. The strengths tended to be the development and coherence of the strategy. The major weaknesses across the sector were:*
> - *Limited reference to the setting of targets for students from non-traditional groups*
> - *Little linkage to other institutional policies*
> - *Limited reference to retention*
> - *Lack of clarity over monitoring arrangements.*
>
> (Action on Access, 2000)

In 2001 HEIs were asked for widening participation strategies (HEFCE, 2001a) that set out plans, targets and activities to cover a three-year period up to 2004. In the accompanying guide to good practice (HEFCE, 2001b) HEIs were advised that widening participation strategies should be holistic in focus, linked to other institutional strategies, and become an integral part of corporate strategies.

Being part of the corporate strategy removes the 'bolt on' marginal feel and provides much greater opportunity for real change from a holistic perspective of linking participation, learning and teaching and employability in an integral manner. HE providers may feel the need for action plans and policy within the corporate strategy that address inclusivity but these need to be firmly lodged within the concept of the student life-cycle as shown in Figure 5, and this requires attention to student need. The challenge here is to ensure that learning and teaching strategies take into account the starting point of the learner as well as the point we wish them to reach by the end of the course.

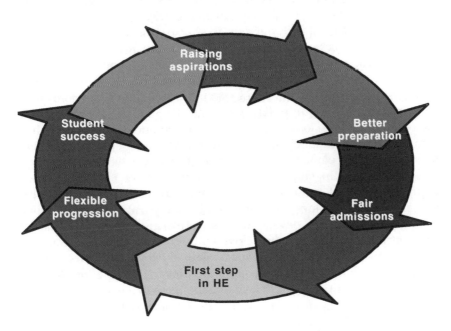

Figure 5: Student life-cycle (Source: HEFCE, 2003a).

The two key government initiatives, OFFA and Aimhigher, have yet to deliver any real change in participation or student success. Aimhigher has the challenging role of building capacity amongst young people to study in HE and therefore the real impact will not be seen for a few years. OFFA does not have any effect until 2006 and its focus is about 'regulating' student bursaries and not changing participation. As indicated earlier, neither of these initiatives actually look at what happens in HE and the focus is solely on getting there!

The institutional response

Universities and colleges respond to the widening participation agenda in very different ways and there are papers in this volume looking at those responses in more detail. In this section I will seek to create a framework to consider how universities and colleges position themselves or to reflect how others may perceive their position. This is, of course, fraught with difficulty, tension and oversimplification.

Many of the Russell Group and the 94 Group of universities that regard themselves as 'research-intensive' have a particular background. Relatively, they have below-average participation from lower socio-economic groups, less than 80 per cent intake from state schools, low numbers of mature students, and lower proportions of home students from minority ethnic groups (HEFCE, HESA Performance Indicators). On the other hand they do have excellent retention and success rates. Their commitment to widening participation is to provide support and routes to enable young people from low-income groups to achieve at the appropriate level and to enter HE at that university or elsewhere. Their approach is one of regional and civic commitment to raising participation and attainment levels and does not have a particular focus on their own supply chain. The development of compact schemes is a particular component of such approaches, along with relatively high bursaries and scholarships, with a recognition that a relatively small percentage will be entitled to such support and therefore the university can afford to pay.

The pre-1992 universities that sit outside these groups generally have a more mixed response between aspects of the research-intensive approach linked to strategies to provide broader opportunities and more of a focus on the supply chain. These universities will have a mixture of recruiting and selecting courses, and will reflect that mix within their approaches.

The new universities are not a homogeneous group and they vary between those that have demonstrably 'raised their entry standards' since 1992 and those that are seeking to provide more open access.

Interestingly, the latter are often criticised for their poor retention rates but on further analysis (Allen, 2004) it is evident that it is not the lower socio-economic groups that are failing or dropping out in those universities but more often those from 'better off' families who did not achieve well at A-level. This may reflect a distinction between A-level performance of individuals who had achieved the best they could as against the best that could be achieved in that educational setting.

The general colleges of HE tend to have strong recruitment from under-represented groups (except in respect of ethnicity) and have strong retention rates based on the culture of small, supportive and friendly organisations.

Colleges of FE again have a varied position depending upon the type of provision they offer and proximity to a university. This reflects the supply chain, the position of local HEIs and subject specialism.

Specialist HE colleges are difficult to analyse in this way given their differences, but they generally perform well in terms of retention and have a mixed student population.

One of the least developed analyses concerning participation is whether or to what extent there is an impact on the performance of an HEI by the region in which it is located. Such an analysis is fraught with difficulties due to 'local' travel across regional boundaries, the disparate nature of some regions, the differential nature of local/national recruitment in certain types of university and the unique position of London. However, examination of the performance indicators (HEFCE, 2001–2003; HESA, 2004) relating to participation from lower socio-economic groups does produce interesting issues. For example, if we look at the South East and South West, utilising sector trends such as the average for the region compared to the UK average, we see a trend showing regional differences as seen in Figure 6.

This is more evident when we look at a comparison between the North West and Yorkshire and the Humber (Figure 7), where there is differential performance. Indeed, rather than measuring against the UK average the trend begins to ask the question of whether the assessment of institutions should be against the *regional* average. This raises issues and questions concerning comparative data: clearly there is a regional factor.

In all areas the universities and colleges are working together in Aimhigher partnerships. They bring different things to the table, as they do in Lifelong Learning Networks (LLNs). This needs to be recognised but it also needs to be addressed in the institutional corporate strategy. The tension between competition and collaboration faces all of the institutions and again the policy drive is conflicting: Aimhigher calls for partnership, OFFA leads to individual sustainability policies, LLNs focus on partnership. There is a danger that within these approaches we forget

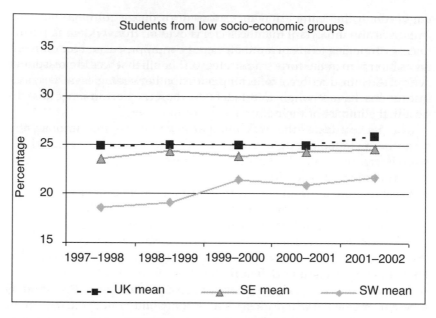

Source: HEFCE Performance Indicator tables (1996 (97) to 2001(02))

Figure 6: South East and South West compared to national means

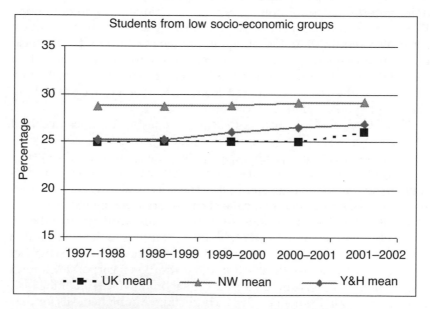

Source: HEFCE Performance Indicator tables (1996 (97) to 2001(02))

Figure 7: North West and Yorkshire & the Humber compared to national means

the needs of the learner and focus too much on institutional perspectives. It is also important that the sector moves on from widening participation strategies to ensuring that there is an appropriate commitment and action plan in the corporate strategy. After all, that was the reasoning behind the introduction of widening participation strategies in 2001, and institutions have enough trend data to monitor performance and to review the impact of their efforts.

In order to address the widening participation agenda seriously the sector needs to look at:

- widening participation approaches that are holistic;
- campaigning for an effective impartial guidance service;
- creating learner progression entitlements;
- celebrating vocational routes;
- recognising diversity.

There is also a need to recognise that institutions and subject disciplines will have their own agendas and needs. Increasingly, the tension between partnerships and individual sustainability of action will come to the fore.

References

Action on Access (2000) *An Analysis of Widening Participation Strategies*, Bradford: Action on Access.

Action on Access (2002) *An Analysis of Widening Participation Strategies*, Bradford: Action on Access.

Coffield, F (1999) *Breaking the Consensus: Lifelong learning as social control*, Inaugural Lecture, University of Newcastle-upon-Tyne.

Dawkins, J (1988) *Higher Education: A Policy Statement*, Canberra: Australia Government Publishing Service.

DEET (1990) *A Fair Chance for All*, Canberra: Australia Government Publishing Service.

DfEE (Department for Education and Employment), (1998) *The Learning Age: a renaissance for a new Britain*, Cm 3790, London: Stationery Office.

DfEE (Department for Education and Employment) (2000) *3rd Report of the National Skills Task Force*, London: DfEE .

DfES (Department for Education and Skills) (2003a) *21st Century Skills: Realising Our Potential*, Cm 5810, London: Stationery Office.

DfES (Department for Education and Skills) (2003b) *The Future of Higher Education*, CM 5735, London: Stationery Office.

DfES (Department for Education and Skills) (2003c) *Widening Participation in Higher Education*, Sheffield: DfES publications.

DfES (Department for Education and Skills) (2005a) *Skills: Getting on in business, getting on at work*, London: Stationery Office.

DfES (Department for Education and Skills) (2005b) *14–19 Education and Skills*, London: Stationery Office.

Field, J (2005) 'Widening access and diversity of provision: The expansion of short cycle higher education in non-university settings', in G Layer (ed), *Closing the Equity Gap: The impact of widening participation strategies in the UK and the USA*, Leicester: NIACE.

HEFCE (Higher Education Funding Council for England) (2000) *Funding for Widening Participation in Higher Education: New Proposals 2000/01*, Circular 00/50 2003/04, Bristol: HEFCE.

HEFCE (Higher Education Funding Council for England) (2001a) *Widening Participation Funding Decisions for 2001/02 – 2003/04*, Circular 01/29, Bristol: HEFCE.

HEFCE (Higher Education Funding Council for England) (2001b) *Strategies for widening participation in higher education: a guide to good practice*, Circular 01/36 June, Bristol: HEFCE.

HEFCE (Higher Education Funding Council for England) (2001c) *Supply and Demand in Higher Education*, Circular 01/02, Bristol: HEFCE.

HEFCE (Higher Education Funding Council for England) (2003a) *Strategic Plan 2003-08*, Circular 03/12, Bristol: HEFCE.

HEFCE (Higher Education Funding Council for England) (2003b) *Performance indicators in Higher Education in the UK 2000–01, 2001–02* and *'A guide to the performance indicators'*, Bristol: HEFCE.

HEFCE (Higher Education Funding Council for England) (200) *Lifelong Learning Networks*, June 2004 Circular 12/04, Bristol: HEFCE.

HESA (Higher Education Statistics Agency) (2004), *Performance Indicators in Higher Education in the UK 2002/03*, Cheltenham: HESA.

Higher Education Act 2004, London: Stationery Office.

Layer, G (2004) *Widening Participation and Employability*, York: LTSN.

McCormick, A (2005) 'Access to Where? Access to What? Towards a comprehensive assessment education' in G Layer (ed), *Closing the Equity Gap: The impact of widening participation strategies in the UK and the USA*, Leicester: NIACE.

Newby, H (2004) 'Doing widening participation: Social inequality and access to higher education', Colin Bell Memorial Lecture, online at:
    http://www.hefce.ac.uk/news/events/2004/bell/bell.doc and in G Layer (ed), *Closing the Equity Gap: The impact of widening participation strategies in the UK and the USA*, Leicester: NIACE.

Parry, G (2005) 'English higher education and near universal access: The college contribution', in G Layer (ed), *Closing the Equity Gap: The impact of widening participation strategies in the UK and the USA*, Leicester: NIACE.

Schuller, T (1997) 'Relations between human and social capital', in *A National Strategy for Lifelong Learning*, Newcastle, 113–25.

Schwartz, S (2004) *Fair Admissions to Higher Education: Recommendations for Good Practice*, Nottingham: DfES.

Stuart, M (2005) 'What price inclusion? Debates and discussions about learning and teaching to widen participation in higher education' in G Layer (ed), *Closing the Equity Gap: The impact of widening participation strategies in the UK and the USA*, Leicester: NIACE.

2

C is for College, for Collaboration, and Creativity: some SCOP[1] reflections on widening participation

Dianne Willcocks

From *Elitism to Inclusion* describes Newman College in the West Midlands as:

a small college making a major contribution to reducing the shortage of ethnic minority teachers and opening up higher education to Birmingham's ethnic communities with the support of the LEA. There is a strong new technology dimension, including the creation of an access community on the internet.

This Inner City Network Community Project illustrates the distinctive role of a mission-led HEI in engaging with locally defined and specific imperatives to widen participation. (CVCP, 1998).

For the past quarter of a century, and under governments of widely differing education principles and priorities, the clarion call to widen participation has exhorted a differentially responsive sector to 'act now!' Specific arguments have shifted over the period, but they are firmly rooted in that time-honoured claim from the 1960s that *a higher education place should be made available to* all *who might benefit* (Robbins, 1963). And so the doors of higher education have been opened: in some cases creakily; in some cases partially; and, in many cases, letting into higher education men and women from communities for whom higher education might have seemed a distant and highly doubtful dream.

Within British higher education we acknowledge that there is diversity of tradition and diversity of mission among universities – some might say a hierarchy. Equally, there is evidence to demonstrate a differential contribution to widening participation, as exemplified by the Higher Education Funding Council for England (HEFCE) performance indicators. What may be less apparent is the particular role and contribution made by the colleges of higher education – that part of the HE community which designates itself as committed to 'dynamic diversity'.

Colleges of higher education are undergoing something of a makeover. That group of HEIs typically referred to as the SCOP sector (Standing Conference of Principals) is both a unified and highly differentiated group of colleges and specialist institutions. A commonality of vision and purpose is shared by clusters of general colleges; visual and performing arts colleges; colleges for the land-based industries; colleges with substantial proportions of teacher education – and a cross-cutting group of church colleges. The geographical spread is wide, with an important presence serving rural communities. And the colleges provide for 1 in 10 students across the whole sector – with a strong emphasis on vocation and/or employability.

The fact that the colleges remain disproportionately attractive to potential students (applications for 2005 increased by 18.5 per cent compared to a sector average of 8.6 per cent, (UCAS, 2005)) hints at the possibility of a key role in widening participation. Excellence in learning and teaching is evidenced in the 2005 successes of colleges in winning CETL status (HEFCE awarded Centres for Excellence in Teaching and Learning). Accordingly, the higher education (HE) colleges and specialist institutions are well-placed to meet, with confidence, the needs of communities of learners who traditionally have failed to secure full advantage from recent HE expansion.

> Innovative practice within a culture of promoting access characterises the institutional learning philosophy. At York St John College, two-thirds of students in arts come from the region; 10 per cent from areas of intense deprivation; 9 per cent with disclosed disabilities. Gweno Williams was awarded a National Teaching Fellowship for her internationally recognised and pioneering approaches to student peer-learning and team development in the arts. Interdisciplinary undergraduate teams act in and produce digital video productions of plays by seventeenth-century women dramatists. These world premier creative outputs, available on DVD as *Margaret Cavendish: Plays in Performance*, offer study materials for higher education worldwide (cited in SCOP, 2004).

One aspect of the dynamic quality of colleges is that the boundaries for this group are themselves fluid. At the start of 2005 there were 54 higher education colleges in the UK (42 in England, six in Scotland, four in Wales and two in Northern Ireland). Of these, 11 were designated university colleges, awarding their own taught degrees. By the end of 2005, numbers will have shifted as a result of eight colleges gaining university title under the 2004 arrangements; one under an earlier regime acquiring powers to award research degrees; and two colleges merging. Two further mergers of colleges may be anticipated in the near future; and further shifts to university status might be anticipated over time. This ability of the colleges to secure advancement and to present themselves as attractive partners to prestigious 'others' suggests that their descriptor of 'dynamic diversity' is multi-faceted and real – and embodies a capacity both to shape and respond to the contemporary higher education agenda.

One particular success factor that colleges claim is a distinctive role among the best of the 'widening participation' providers and a proven track record in enabling participation for new generations of learners – at the same time as demonstrating learning-led excellence linked to scholarship and research. The ethos of these (comparatively) small establishments is one in which attention to the individual combined with a strong sense of community creates secure yet challenging space for those who lack confidence in their own capability and credibility as learners.

So what is the evidence base for SCOP 'performance' in widening participation? Essentially, this may be gleaned from a judicious mix of the HEFCE published performance indicators alongside a rich mix of case study material. Importantly, I am arguing that SCOP colleges have a distinctive – but not necessarily unique – role in attracting and supporting new communities of learners. All HEIs can, and many do, engage with new kinds of learners – some managing higher levels of risk than others. What has been deemed to matter, and what informs the regulatory regime at OFFA (Office for Fair Access), is that the particular strengths of different parts of the HE sector are directed towards that which they best might contribute to the widening-participation mix.

An examination of HEFCE data offers some interesting insights (a statistical digest is appended). The most recent published data show that the SCOP colleges are more likely than universities to admit state school entrants and that they tend to draw them disproportionately from low-participation neighbourhoods – both for first degrees and for foundation degrees. Colleges also accept more students in receipt of Disabled Students' Allowance. It is pleasing to note that good performance by this sub-sector in terms of participation is also reflected across the student life-cycle with good retention and good learning outcomes. Colleges also perform above benchmark for first-destination achievement.

A Scottish example of practice excellence exemplifies key relationships that help to shape effective participation in Glasgow – a city of cultural contrasts. *Glasgow School of Art is one of the UK's most prestigious art schools, offering a unique accredited 'artists in residence' scheme to attract pupils from the poorest schools in Glasgow to the study of art in general and to the school of art in particular. This scheme recognises and encourages potential through a flexible admissions system, which seeks a 10 per cent baseline increase across the institution in participation by lower socio-economic groups.* This demonstrates the importance of specific local targeting which is geared both to population profile and to supplying skills for the city's increasingly significant cultural industries sector (cited in Universities UK, 2002, the following report to CVCP, 1998, *From elitism to inclusion*)

Arguably, the colleges of higher education play a full role both in responding to the widening-participation agenda – which they have delivered through a combination of creativity and collaborative endeavour – and in shaping the forward agenda – where they can play a pivotal role. Much of this is embedded in the mission and *modus operandi* of such institutions, which can be traced, in many instances, to political struggle and educational reform in the nineteenth century leading to a very early articulation of access – albeit, not bearing that nomenclature.

Education reform in Victorian England was enacted across complex and contested territory. New kinds of institutions were created to meet the needs of what were primarily new and urban poor working-class communities. For example, a significant cluster of church colleges was sponsored by dioceses to train teachers for the new church schools that were themselves designed to widen education opportunity for the masses. Craft and technical institutes were likewise sponsored within the burgeoning municipalities to promote skills and (modest) enlightenment for the respectable working man. The impact of industrialisation promoted a further concern for the changing nature of the countryside – and a reciprocal response in formation of educational institutes for agricultural workers facing new challenges.

It is within this dynamic and uncharted context that the colleges of higher education and specialist institutions laid the foundations for creating learning opportunity by linking education and training programmes with a range of new beneficiaries in different situations. In particular, there was strong representation in provincial (cathedral) cities and rural environments alongside a responsiveness to need generated by rapid urban and industrial expansion. These traditions of active engagement with social and economic change inform the values base and infuse the ethos of today's HE colleges.

Clearly, a century and a half of educational change and development, accelerating particularly over the past 50 years, has left its mark on the colleges. Where the pattern of change differs from that of universities is that colleges are significantly reduced in number and scale overall. Yet they are strengthened, like other HEIs, in terms of the quality of output; their present viability; and their continuing engagement with respect to a wider public expectation for social, economic and cultural contribution. Colleges (particularly church colleges) are well placed to inform present debates around ethics and values for a modern global society. A particular example of contemporary engagement is the concern for environmental matters and global sustainability. In the recent (2005) HEFCE consultation on sustainability it is, perhaps, no coincidence that three out of four case studies highlighted at regional meetings showed two colleges and a former college (now university) presenting cutting-edge examples of HE leadership for environmental policy, practice and research.[2]

What is curious about the colleges sub-sector, given a defensible pride in history and tradition, is the ease with which it has tended to allow what might be termed the tyranny of hierarchies – a less-than-positive aspect of British society and culture – to downplay its past and present contribution to sector change and enhancement. It is helpful to explore how some present hierarchical dysfunctions in HE tend to exacerbate this situation. For example, many commentators endorse without question a concept of institutional diversity that embraces the phrase 'our best universities' – without ever defining or justifying 'best for what or for whom'. Equally, we have engaged in a fair admissions debate that is predicated on the directing of A-level students to the 'best' university of their choice – paying scant attention to the rich mix of entrants and expectations. We fail to challenge adequately an approach to HE policy where the 'boarding school' model persists –three-year, full-time, residential and on-campus. We have yet to fully acknowledge or calibrate learning-in-the-workplace. And we have a tradition of complaining about inappropriate (non-valid) league tables – yet exploiting ferociously those which favour our own institutions[3] and much more.

Various government policies and initiatives have sought to tackle this dilemma and argue the case for equity or efficiency linked with diversity in the distribution of educational benefit – yet hierarchy persists, often seen as a rational approach to achieving equity and efficiency! So, different stakeholders construct, more or less explicitly, hierarchies of institutions; hierarchies of HE entrants; hierarchies of subjects – and, most problematic of all, hierarchies of communities (where the latter may interact with the rest). By illustration, we have yet to debate fully the acceptability of policy predicated on the following: research-intensive universities as natural leaders in the institutional ranks; gifted and talented A level entrants being seen as the primary link in the higher education 'supply chain'; STEM (Science, Technology, Engineering and Mathematics) subjects and medicine clearly superseding lesser-regarded vocational and arts programmes. Meanwhile, there is a growing acceptance that the needs of rural and coastal communities for educational investment and skills development continue to be poorly articulated and overshadowed by the highly visible and politicised needs of an urban/metropolitan regeneration agenda. Given geographical location, the contribution of HE colleges to re-balancing these latter expressions of interest and responses to need can be powerful – whether from the land-based colleges or other parts of the college mix.

> In the most recent HEIF (Higher Education Innovation Fund) allocations Harper Adams University College in Shropshire was successful in winning £1.4M from HEFCE to develop work with rural businesses – promoting innovation for sustainable farming and supporting the growth of sustainable technologies and the improvement of food chain safety. This grant will also help to expand the work of WIRE – Women In Rural Enterprise – a business club supporting more than 1,500 businesswomen across the UK.

The focus of government commitment to widening participation over the past decade has been predicated on achieving 50 per cent participation for young HE entrants and a greater working-class representation. Associated with this is the principle of requiring students to invest in their higher education whilst introducing mechanisms that aim to promote fair access. There has been endorsement for work-relevant foundation degrees and a shift towards regional responsiveness. This in turn has led to closer work with Regional Development Agencies; the development of more flexible partnerships across further and higher education; an increasing focus on sub-regions; and a refinement of work with young people to specify goals for aspiration-raising, attainment and achievement, leading to educational progression and a more explicit and robust framework for lifelong learning. Importantly, there has been a significant and supportive voice from SCOP and from the individual colleges in shaping this policy-practice continuum. Yet the outcomes remain problematic.

The impact of intervention to date is at best partial with respect to the 'big questions' of meaningful accessibility for the new widening participation learners we seek. Continued insistence on the A-level 'gold standard' could be interpreted as militating against the success of vocational progression strategies. Of particular concern to colleges has been the narrow debate around fair access, which gives emphasis to enlargement of the applicant pool – but is then focused on moving 'the best' applicants around the system more effectively; in this dialogue, vocational routes have been largely ignored. And the introduction of variable fees coupled with deferred payment might prove attractive to some student communities, but it may well deter others. So, we in the colleges sector will gear up for a more intensive summer 'clearance sale' in August 2006. But with pre-emptive price adjustments from a selection of HEIs already in the public domain, a future higher education 'blue cross day' might not be too fanciful!

Nevertheless, progress continues: two initiatives that cautiously herald promise are Aimhigher and the presently-evolving Lifelong Learning Networks (LLNs). The colleges of higher education have taken a leading role at both regional and sub-regional level to ensure that we realise fully the potential for investment in genuine 'widening' that is offered by these mechanisms. First, Aimhigher outreach (growing out of Excellence in Cities and Partnerships for Progression) seeks to create cultural shifts and changed educational behaviours with respect to HE entry. Second, LLNs, are charged with introducing delivery arrangements across a cluster of further/ higher education providers, with each partnership being required to include at least one research-intensive university; these will major on flexible and transparent progression for vocational learners.

HE colleges have engaged positively with their university partners and local agencies to ensure LLN success. In particular, SCOP and its member HEIs have been consistent in giving voice to the urgent need for more appropriate arrangements (financial, regulatory and representational) to bridge the further and higher education divide – both with respect to the valued role of FE in HE and in order to promote flexible vocational progression. However, the outreach agenda remains a significant challenge, with HE colleges active in seeking local solutions. Notwithstanding present financial challenges for Aimhigher, the capacity that has been built for raising aspirations and achievement levels is substantial. Increasingly, this must be linked with local progression arrangements that map flexible journeys (individualised learning plans) to signpost and support the vocational learner – who will follow programmes of study which are themselves shaped by a modern sense of curriculum.

The role which colleges have played in challenging the academic/ vocational divide is unquestionable. Indeed, in a real sense this was part of the original philosophy and mission of many of our institutions. Innovative approaches to curriculum content, design and delivery patterns have, over a number of years, tended to dissolve this hierarchical division. Meanwhile, the government, other parts of the sector and the media continue to describe HE based on what may be a shrinking tradition. Arguably this reality gap arises through lack of visibility for the college contribution and a pre-occupation with traditional (elitist) models of knowledge, skills and achievement. Curiously, the shift for a limited number of erstwhile colleges to become the next generation of universities may secure a new dialogue around widening participation realities – just as this move vindicates the quality of the HE experience that they and other SCOP colleges have engendered.

This connects to a further dimension of widening participation that has, perhaps, failed to secure full recognition to-date and that is the relationship with definitions of quality. We, in SCOP, have made the case that understandings of the quality of the learner experience must embrace value-added in terms of widening participation – rather than focusing on research ratings and/or input measures such as A-level points. Given recent and related expansion/modernisation in higher education the issue of quality risk management has come to the fore with respect to new kinds of learners and new kinds of learning.[4] It has been part of the historic mission of the colleges to demonstrate that added-value in terms of output/process measures serves as a more powerful driver for quality than some kind of value-maintenance which is inherently risk averse.

In conclusion, this paper seeks to align dynamic shifts in widening participation work over the recent period with shifts in the profile of colleges as they emerge to claim more explicitly their appropriate place in policy and practice formation. It argues that the traditions of the colleges and specialist institutions have exerted a powerful influence on widening participation policy and good practice. Looking to the future, our track record in collaborating with diverse agencies, alongside the forging of creative solutions with partners, augurs well for continuing moves towards equity and engagement in higher education for that wider community of beneficiaries.

Performance indicators in higher education in the UK, 2002–2003
Analysis of HE college performance[5]

English institutions only

Strong performances
Projected Learning Outcomes (Table 5)
Full-Time students starting first degree courses (2001/02)

	Percentage of colleges	Percentage of universities
Degree		
Met or exceeded HEI benchmark	69	59
Met or exceeded UK average (77.9 %)	58	56
Met or exceeded English average (78.4 %)	58	54
Percentage of mature starters	69	54

Participation of under-represented groups in HE (Table 1a)
Young full-time first degree entrants (2002/03)

	Percentage of colleges	Percentage of universities
State school or college		
Met or exceeded HEI benchmark	82	64
Met or exceeded UK average (87.2 %)	87	58
Met or exceeded English average (86.4 %)	87	58
NS-SEC classes 4,5, 6 & 7		
Met or exceeded HEI benchmark	63	56
Met or exceeded UK average (28.4 %)	83	51
Met or exceeded English average (27.9 %)	83	52
From low-participation neighbourhoods		
Met or exceeded HEI benchmark	58	49
Met or exceeded UK average (13.3 %)	48	35
Met or exceeded English average (12.5 %)	55	39

Participation of under-represented groups in HE (Table 1b)
Young full-time undergraduate entrants including Foundation Degree, HND (2002/03)

	Percentage of colleges	Percentage of universities
Met or exceeded HEI benchmark	84	64
Met or exceeded UK average (87.8 %)	87	57
Met or exceeded English average (86.9 %)	87	58

	Percentage of colleges	Percentage of universities
NS-SEC classes 4,5, 6 & 7		
Met or exceeded HEI benchmark	60	51
Met or exceeded UK average (29.2 %)	74	51
Met or exceeded English average (28.6 %)	80	51
From low participation neighbourhoods		
Met or exceeded HEI benchmark	50	45
Met or exceeded UK average (13.9 %)	45	31
Met or exceeded English average (13 %)	50	36

Participation of students in receipt of DSA (Table 7)
Full-time first degree and all undergraduate students (2002/03)

	Percentage of colleges	Percentage of universities
Full-time first degree		
Met or exceeded HEI benchmark	55	39
Met or exceeded UK and English average (2.6 %)	70	41
Full-time all undergraduates		
Met or exceeded HEI benchmark	55	38
Met or exceeded UK or English average (2.5 %)	70	39
Part-time all undergraduates		
Met or exceeded HEI benchmark	44	41
Met or exceeded UK average (1.3%)	44	26
Met or exceeded English average (0.9%)	63	42

Participation of under-represented groups in HE (Table 2b)
Part-Time undergraduate entrants (2002/03)
(No previous HE and from low-participation neighbourhoods)

	Percentage of colleges	Percentage of universities
All entrants		
Met or exceeded HEI benchmark	48	47
Met or exceeded UK average (8.3 %)	36	21
Met or exceeded English average (7.9 %)	44	24
Young undergraduate		
Met or exceeded HEI benchmark	60	42
Met or exceeded UK average (20.5 %)	30	28
Met or exceeded English average (17.7 %)	60	36
Mature undergraduate		
Met or exceeded HEI benchmark	46	47
Met or exceeded UK average (7.6 %)	38	24
Met or exceeded English average (7.4 %)	38	25

Non-continuation following year of entry (Table 3a)
Full-Time first degree entrants 2001/02
Percentage of institutions where proportion of students no longer in HE:

	Percentage of colleges	Percentage of universities
Mature		
Met or exceeded HEI benchmark	59	59
Met or exceeded UK average (14.9 %)	71	61
Met or exceeded English average (14.8 %)	71	59

Satisfactory performances
Participation of under-represented groups in HE (Table 2a)
Mature full-time undergraduate entrants (2002/03)
No previous HE and from low-participation neighbourhoods

	Percentage of colleges	Percentage of universities
Met or exceeded HEI benchmark	47	41
Met or exceeded UK average (15.4 %)	31	40
Met or exceeded English average (15 %)	36	40

Non-continuation following year of entry (Table 3a)
Full-Time first degree entrants 2001/02
Percentage not in HE

	Percentage of colleges	Percentage of universities
All entrants		
Met or exceeded HEI benchmark	62	60
Met or exceeded UK average (9 %)	41	57
Met or exceeded English average (8.7 %)	36	53
Young entrants		
Met or exceeded HEI benchmark	64	59
Met or exceeded UK average (7.3 %)	36	51
Met or exceeded English average (7 %)	33	51

Non-continuation following year of entry (Table 3c)
Mature full-time first degree entrants (2001/02)
Percentage not in HE

	Percentage of colleges	Percentage of universities
No previous HE qualification		
Met or exceeded HEI benchmark	53	54
Met or exceeded UK and English average (14.9%)	67	56

Notes

1. Standing Conference of Principals.
2. Surrey Institute of Art & Design University College; York St John College; and University of Gloucestershire
3. SCOP has now acted to challenge media 'ownership' of league table concepts and data via Yorke and Longden, 2005.
4. This is explored most powerfully in Raban and Turner, 2005.
5. SCOP, 2004.

References

CVCP (1998) *From Elitism to Inclusion: Good practice in widening access to higher education,* Committee of Vice Chancellors and Principals.

Raban, C and Turner, E (2005) *Managing Academic Risk,* Bristol: HEFCE.

Robbins, L (1963) *Higher Education: Report of the Committee,* London: HMSO.

SCOP (2004) *Sustainability for Success: SCOP submission to Government Spending Review.*

UCAS (2005) *Applications Digest.*

Universities UK (2002) *Social Class and Participation: good practice in widening access to higher education.*

Yorke, M and Longden, B (2005) *Significant Figures: Performance Indicators and 'League Tables',* SCOP.

3
Widening participation and research-intensive universities – A contradiction in terms?

Mary Stuart

> *The last frontier of participation in higher education ...refers to the social class mix. ...the gap in participation rates between the top and bottom socio-economic classes has moved only slightly*
>
> (Newby, 2005a: 5).

There is no doubt that Russell Group institutions, which are considered to be the most prestigious institutions in the UK, do not attract students from low socio-economic groups.[1] So perhaps there is no need to expand any further. Perhaps that is it. We should recognise that widening participation cannot be, and is not, a feature of such institutions. The HE sector is increasingly differentiated and perhaps widening participation should be left to those who are 'good at it'. But, as Duke points out this is not a simple matter:

> *Differentiation within the sector is getting sharper, but not in useful and complementary ways. A hard-won place in the new, 'mainly teaching' university may be devalued by competitive abuse, one-dimensional league tables and talk of plunging standards*
>
> (Duke, 2005: 3).

Hence perceptions of widening access are tied up in a sort of snobbish elitism which affects the opinion of the wider public. Differentiation is, therefore, a double-edged sword. There are several questions that need further investigation in looking at widening participation and research intensity, such as: 'Can you equate research intensity with a particular group of institutions such as the Russell Group?' and 'Is research intensity to be equated with "good universities"?' We also need to ask if a focus on teaching really enables widening participation and, in the search for social equity, can certain institutions, often defined as 'elite', be ignored, while others provide learning opportunities for working-class students?

In trying to answer these questions we need to examine the taken-for-granted everyday attitudes about higher education. This chapter is about perceptions: perceptions about research intensity, perceptions about widening participation and, of course, perceptions about higher education. It questions the position taken by some that achieving widening participation will happen through conventional student achievement and gold standard performance. I argue that a focus on curriculum development is potentially a more fruitful way of widening access and creating more equal social outcomes. I start by examining the UK government's perceptions of the widening participation problem.

'Excellence' and equity – perceptions of government

In 1999 the government announced the 'Excellence Challenge', a programme of school improvement centred on cohorts of young people from disadvantaged neighbourhoods at inner city schools in England. It ignored large areas of disadvantage across England, including areas of rural and coastal poverty. It also ignored adult disadvantage, and focused on broadly defined catchment areas, sometimes allocating funds to successful middle-class schools as well as schools with high proportions of working-class students. The programme drew in a range of higher education institutions providing additional support for the young people in these schools, including offering residential summer schools at universities for students completing their compulsory education in year 11. Most of the HEIs who were invited to participate in these programmes were from the old-established university sector, mostly Russell Group institutions. The whole programme was premised on a conventional gold standard route into higher education, i.e. straight through from school into A-levels and on to university.

Since 1999, when the programme was launched, Russell Group institutions' performance indicators for widening access have remained below benchmark by scores between 0.3 to 6.3, with Oxford and Cambridge being furthest away from the benchmark, Southampton coming a close third and institutions like Bristol still being 6 points off their benchmark.[2] This information indicates that despite considerable government funds, both from Excellence Challenge and later Aim Higher, as well as specific funds to encourage more state school entrants into such institutions, there has been little progress. To be fair, progress in this area takes time. It is unlikely that you will be able to change the attitudes and performance of pupils overnight. Apart from summer schools, many of the initiatives to widen participation in HE focused on young people starting the GCSE curriculum and since these initiatives started there have only been three cohorts who could have moved into HE. However, governments are renowned for being impatient and our current government is no different.

More recently, institutions had the opportunity to address their equity targets through their Office for Fair Access (OFFA) agreements, but an initial analysis of these agreements suggests that Russell Group institutions have not introduced targets to improve their recruitment of students from low socio-economic backgrounds into their agreements. Rather than using these Access agreements as an opportunity to create positive outcomes, they have focused on activities without measuring the effects of these actions. Many would argue that all of this is not surprising and would suggest that research intensity and widening participation simply will never co-exist. However, before we accept the perception of the Russell Group as simply research intensive perhaps we should examine the ideal of research intensity in more detail.

Measuring intensity

Nearly all HEIs engage in research and would defend its importance for the sector. When the research assessment exercise (RAE) was introduced, it quickly became a selectivity exercise concentrating funds in certain institutions. Measures of research intensity are often challenged and contested. It is possible to examine the statistics from the last RAE, although given the length of time between assessments; we know that there is considerable movement of staff, suggesting that the statistics could be out of date. As well as this, the RAE only measures a small proportion of research activity. We could use different measures. We could choose to examine overall research volume, another way of defining 'intensity', but this will not tell us about the quality of the research undertaken. On the other hand many universities score very highly on applied research for business and social purposes which could act as a measure of 'socially robust knowledge' (Gibbons, 2005: 1). Others would argue that so-called 'blue-sky' research is essential for the development of new ways of thinking. Whatever measure is chosen, there are complexities in defining what is meant by research intensity and even if one accepts the conventional RAE definitions there are a variety of possible results which is worth explaining further.

Unsurprisingly, if we take research intensity as over 90 per cent of staff from an institution submitted to the last exercise and over 30 per cent of submissions gaining a 5 star rating, the usual suspects emerge;

Cambridge, Oxford, Southampton, Imperial, the LSE and UCL. However, Lancaster is also in this league. If you take a broader definition of
say at least 90 per cent of staff submitted and 90 per cent of submissions
gaining a 4 or above, a different list develops including Royal Holloway,
York, Warwick, Sussex and UMIST as well as the others listed above. On
the other hand, other members of the Russell Group, Bristol and
Liverpool to take two examples, only submitted 88 per cent and 83 per
cent of their staff respectively. While I would not want to suggest that
these institutions are not highly research active, I would argue that definitions are complex and difficult to pin down. However, measures such
as the RAE create particular results, not only in terms of the league tables,
but also in funding, as Watson points out; 'the expanding differential
between funding research and funding teaching ...in England seems
inexorable' (2005a: 40).

Discussions about the RAE and particular measures for research are
of particular interest to the HE community, and in examining the question of whether widening participation and research intensity can sit
alongside each other, it is important to look beyond such internal debates
to the public at large and their perceptions of universities.

Are research-intensive universities 'good' universities? The public's perceptions

Perceptions of what a good university is seem to relate, but not equate,
to research intensity. For example in a recent *Times Higher Education
Supplement* (2005), students perceived the following institutions as being
strong in league tables: Oxford, Cambridge, Bristol, York, St Andrews
and Durham. Compared with the definitions produced by the RAE,
where are Southampton, UCL etc. etc.? So while there are some connections between research intensity and being a 'good' university there is
no direct match. In the same survey, students saw 'old universities more
highly rated in terms of academic reputation' (THES, 2005). Yet in quality
assessments many new universities are considered to be excellent at
teaching and of course not all 'old universities' are research intensive in
the definitions cited above. The new National Student Survey, which
measures student perceptions of teaching, will throw up further
complexities in definitions of what a 'good' university is. Even in this
survey there are some interesting issues of measurement. If insufficient
students responded to the survey from any particular institution or
subject area in that institution, the results will not be reported. This
means that there are significant gaps in our knowledge of what students
actually think about teaching in certain HEIs.

Reay, David and Ball (2005) found that students chose universities by what they considered or were told were 'good universities' and institutions that market their offer strongly were thought to be 'getting a bit desperate' (141). One mother of a middle-class student sums up the perception issue:

> In a sense he just knew which the best ones were. And it wasn't the league tables. It's just the sense of the university, the location, the history and just a kind of knowing that people just do know what's good
> (Reay, David and Ball, 2005:67).

Hence at one level the problem is not really about research intensity or teaching quality or even league tables, hard as all these are to define, but about a taken-for-granted sense of an elite within universities that is passed down in a diffuse 'one-knows' way, or in more academic terms, through a process of cultural capital. Bourdieu and Passeron set out the real problem for conventional widening participation as set out by the excellence challenge in this way:

> Depending on whether access to higher education is collectively felt, even in a diffuse way, as an impossible, possible, probable, normal or banal future, everything in the conduct of families and the children (particularly their conduct and performance at school) will vary, because behaviour tends to be governed by what is 'reasonable' to accept
> (1977: 226).

This highlights the real problem. Within families expectations provide the framework for children's performance and their future lives. Constraints on working-class students are enormous. For many, getting the results they need in order to attend certain institutions is difficult. From studies in the UK, it is clear that A-level students from working-class families take on significant amounts of paid employment in order to help their families (Forsyth and Furlong, 2003; Archer *et al*, 2003), which can affect their results. For those who move on to higher-level study, many will study locally because they need to live at home, are expected to live at home or choose to keep part-time employment they need during their time in HE. Studies highlight this as a feature of working-class student life in both the UK (Reay, David and Ball, 2005) and in the USA (McCormick, 2005). This means that, for many students, leafy out-of-town campuses are not a possibility.

Equally, there is evidence that some institutions are simply not seen to be sufficiently friendly to students from low socio-economic groups, for example, Reay, David and Ball quote one such student who chose a new university near her home:

> *I don't see the point in spending my time with people who are not going to be able to relate to me and I'm not going to be able to relate to them. We are from different worlds, so I think I've had enough of that in my life... I don't want to feel as if I have to pretend to be someone I'm not*
>
> (2005: 94).

Perceptions also play a part here. The student knows, in the same way that the mother of the middle-class student knew, what were the 'good universities'. In this case, the 'right' university is one where she will feel comfortable. As Bourdieu and Passeron stated 'behaviour is governed by what is reasonable to accept' (op cit).

Reframing the problem – new universities, new approaches and curricula

However, perhaps the perception of government to create access to 'what is' in HE is misguided in the first place. Historically I would argue that widening access to HE has always depended on the changing needs of society. This has usually entailed new curriculum developments. In the nineteenth century the 'new universities' developed curricula suitable to the developing world of industry and commerce, engineering, the professions, and so on.

These 'new', soon to become 'old', universities, such as Birmingham, Liverpool and Leeds, played a significant role in providing HE provision for working-class students, in their extra-mural departments throughout the twentieth century, but this work was seldom linked to conventional degree programmes. These departments have now almost disappeared (Taylor, 2005), partly because of the growth of part-time adult learning opportunities and new curricula offered by the development of the Open Universities and other new universities, and partly because the agenda for adults has lost favour with government. Taylor points out that these processes militate against adult learners; 'national funding formulae and bureaucratic structures discriminate against adult learning provision' (2005: 30).

Another example of the development of new HE and new curricula emerged in the 1960s. The Robbins Report in 1963 provided a significant expansion of HE provision and the development of new curricula. This created an increase in HE entrance of 50 per cent between 1963 and 1968.

While New Labour has emphasised the importance of widening participation, it is the case that successive governments have expanded and widened HE. For example, in 1987, under a Conservative government, *HE: Meeting the Challenge* paved the way for the expansion of Access programmes (Reay *et al*, 2005). With the increase of nursing and other health-related subjects into universities, the gender gap significantly decreased, and through Access programmes and increases in art and design and related fields women have overtaken men in higher education. If we are to create social equity for working-class students, Newby's final frontier, then new curricula and new ways of working are the main routes we must take. The idea is to develop new curricula that are vocationally relevant to the post-industrial era we find ourselves in and which will attract new learners.

Two strategies have been developed: a new qualification, the Foundation Degree, and new ways of enabling lifelong learning, the Lifelong Learning Network (Newby, 2005b; Watson, 2005b). Higher education colleges are also emerging as important players in this new world. These colleges, many of whom are now seeking university title, are actively developing the vocational HE agenda. They also have a significant part to play in widening participation.

As previously in the history of the development of universities in England, it is the new universities, at any point in time, who have taken on ideas about new curricula. 'Old universities' have been more reluctant to address the new agenda including this time, developing few Foundation Degrees. On reviewing their OFFA statements only one Russell Group institution mentioned Foundation Degrees.

Negative attitudes to vocational education are deep rooted in British society. Archer *et al* eloquently sum-up the difficulties inherent in the vocation/academic divide in the UK:

> *Resistance to vocational education, or to some forms of vocational education, has come from a number of different directions (and goes back before the 19th century)* (my brackets), *including academics on the left of the political spectrum, New Right traditionalists and aspects of the media*
> (2003: 141)

Perceptions are that vocational higher education is not proper HE and if too dominant in their provision, will give the institution a poor reputation. However it was the 'new universities' in the industrial towns in the nineteenth century that established engineering and modern languages degrees. At the time they, too, were thought to be lowering standards, so this is a battle that needs to be fought again. HEFCE has insisted that 'research-intensive' institutions must be involved in Lifelong Learning Networks, and perhaps these new fledgling schemes will offer a chance to really address the problems of social equity in HE, by making HEIs think about curricula and new students in a different way (Layer, 2005).

Willis (2003) argues that young people are in the vanguard of engagement with new technology. They are the first to want and to learn to use these commodities:

Young and working class people are caught up in the front line of engagement. They articulate the materials of commodity culture almost as a matter of cultural life or death, not least because they find themselves with....little or no access to legitimate and bourgeois forms of cultural capital.....In the school this points to the importance of understanding popular cultural consumption...

(405).

His argument that education providers need to address the concerns of young people is not only applicable to the school environment but also to HEIs, where attention needs to be paid to the new digital age, its economic meaning in society, and the resulting changes in curricula and learning practices. It is only with this kind of engagement that we will capture the imagination of young working class people. Frand (2000) argues that there is a new mindset amongst young people. He points out that HEIs need to engage with this new world:

The outlook of those we teach has changed, and thus the way in which we teach must change. The world in which we all live has changed, and thus the content we teach must change. The industrial age has become the information age, and thus the way we organise our institutions must change as must the meaning we attach to the terms 'student' 'teacher' and 'alumni'.

(24).

New curricula and new ways of teaching and learning have always been the domain of the 'new' universities and HEIs. However, while such developments are crucial to both widening participation and the economic development of our society, government perceptions of many such developments, despite the fact that they introduced the Foundation Degree, are that they are 'Mickey Mouse' degrees. This is hugely misguided and yet another perception that needs to be challenged. The question about widening participation and research intensive universities is therefore not the right question. The question should be; can we change the perceptions of what a 'good' university is from a belief that old fashioned is somehow quality and new ideas are somehow common, to a belief that a 'good' university is one that is fit for purpose?

The perception battle, and more significantly, the social processes of stratification, that create these perceptions, have to be fought not only in HEIs but across the whole of society.

Notes

1. All but Birmingham University are below their benchmark for young people from lower socio-economic groups.
2. Figures from HEFCE benchmark for participation by under represented groups in higher education, young full-time degree entrants, 2003. These are the very students targeted by the Excellence Challenge programme.

References

Archer, L, Hutchings, M and Ross, M (2003) *Higher Education and Social Class* London: Routledge Falmer .

Duke, C (2005) 'The crab's progress: approaching a tertiary system for lifelong learning', in C Duke (ed), *The Tertiary Moment: What road to inclusive higher education?* Leicester: NIACE..

Frand, J L (2000) 'The information age: mindset changes in students and implications for higher education', *Educause Review*, Sept/Oct, 15–24.

Gibbons, M (2005) *Engagement with the Community: the emergence of a new social contract between society and science*
   www.griffith.edu.au/txt/er/news/2005_1/michael_gibbons.html.

HEFCE (2001) *2001 Research Assessment Exercise: The Outcome*, December 2001 RAE 4/01.

Layer, G (2005) 'Closing the equity gap – is it sustainable?' in G Layer (ed), *Closing the Equity Gap The impact of widening participation strategies in the UK and the USA*, Leicester: NIACE.

McCormick, A (2005) 'Access where? Access to what? Towards a comprehensive assessment', in G Layer (ed), *Closing the Equity Gap The impact of widening participation strategies in the UK and the USA*, Leicester: NIACE.

Newby H (2005b) 'Lifelong Learning Networks in Higher Education', *Journal of Access Policy and Practice*, vol 2(2), 176–87.

Newby, H (2005a) 'The Colin Bell Memorial Lecture – Doing widening participation: social inequality and access to higher education', in G Layer (ed), *Closing the Equity Gap The impact of widening participation strategies in the UK and the USA*, Leicester: NIACE.

Reay, D, David, M and Ball, S (2005) *Degrees of Choice: Social class, race and gender in higher education*, Stoke-on-Trent: Trentham Books.

Taylor , R (2005) 'Prospects for adult learning in higher education', in C Duke (ed), *The Tertiary Moment: What road to inclusive higher education?* Leicester: NIACE.

Times Higher Education Supplement (2005) *What Impresses Today's Freshers?* 17 June, 2005.

Watson, D (2005a) 'Telling the truth about widening participation', in G Layer (ed), *Closing the Equity Gap The impact of widening participation strategies in the UK and the USA*, Leicester: NIACE.

Watson, D (2005b) 'Will Lifelong Learning Networks work? A perspective from higher education', *Journal of Access Policy and Practice*, vol 2(2), 187–205.

Willis, P (2003) 'Foot soldiers of modernity: the dialectics of cultural consumption of the 21st century', *Harvard Educational Review*, vol 73(3).

4

Implications for the mixed economy group colleges

John Widdowson

Colleges of further education place widening participation by under-represented groups of learners at the centre of their role. Until recently, for many colleges the emphasis has been on preparing learners for employment or for progression to programmes of higher education provided by other institutions. In contrast, for the 'Mixed Economy Group' of colleges the provision of higher education has long been a key feature of their curriculum offer. However, the drive to increase and widen participation has led all colleges to evaluate their contribution and to look for opportunities to build on past success.

New providers of higher education

Wider participation has given many colleges the encouragement to offer a broader range of higher education courses delivered in the college environment. Partnerships with higher education institutions have been essential as colleges seek validation of a range of new programmes, in particular, employer-related Foundation Degrees. Although experience has varied between colleges, there has been a significant increase in the amount of higher education delivered by colleges. The need to develop relationships with HEIs that go beyond simply providing progression pathways for students has given rise to a range of issues. For colleges receiving funding as well as validation services from universities, the nature of that financial relationship has given rise to concern. The lack of robust contractual arrangements has placed considerable strain on some partnerships, resulting in some colleges shifting validation between HEIs.

The Mixed Economy Group

The Mixed Economy Group of colleges (MEG) was formed several years ago to provide a forum for the discussion of issues of relevance to further education colleges directly funded to deliver higher education. From time to time the group has also lobbied funding and regulatory bodies on behalf of the interests of its members. With the recent changes to funding and qualification structures, MEG has taken the opportunity to consider its purpose and structure.

In 2005, the group adopted a statement of purpose which gives prominence to widening participation:

> *The Mixed Economy Group of colleges represents those Further Education colleges which have a strategic role in the provision of programmes of Higher Education.*
> *The Group is committed to:*
> * *Widening participation in Higher Education amongst groups currently underrepresented.*
> * *Promoting the value of vocational Higher Education in raising the aspirations of individuals and meeting the skill needs of the economy.*
> * *Working in partnership to develop and deliver high quality, innovative approaches to Higher Education.*

('Strategic' is defined as having 500 full time equivalent higher education students funded from whatever source).

In terms of curriculum, MEG colleges offer a wide range of provision. Whilst some have a specialism e.g. art and design or land-based industries, the majority offer a broad range of degree and sub degree programmes. Some of these occupy niche markets. MEG members have been early developers and adopters of Foundation Degrees, although with some issues around the impact on learners of a move away from accepted qualifications such as HND. Members are also major providers of 'non-prescribed' HE i.e. those qualifications funded by the Learning and Skills Council leading to the awards of professional bodies or higher level NVQs.

The response from MEG colleges to top-up fees and Access Agreements has been mixed. For directly funded provision, member colleges have adopted a range of responses. Some have proposed to introduce higher fee levels but accompanied by bursaries, which will be either means-tested or available to all students irrespective of means. In many cases, colleges have introduced higher fees not simply to generate revenue but against a competitive market background, to avoid any assumption that a lower fee means lower quality. Others have chosen to await more concrete evidence of the impact of increased fees. Many MEG colleges believe their core provision to be at risk in a much more competitive environment. Maintaining lower fees levels is seen as one strategy to attract students for whom the prospect of debt may be a real disincentive to participation. For most students studying in a further education college, the choice to do so is a positive one and not simply the result of having failed to gain a place elsewhere.

Who are the students?

At a time of change it can be dangerous to generalise about the characteristics of students currently choosing to study for higher level awards in the further education sector. Indeed, where colleges offer provision aimed at niche markets, any generalisations may by definition be less true. However, students who do choose an FE college as their place of study may share one or more of a range of factors.

Many will come from families with no direct experience or involvement in higher education and may be the first from that family to consider HE. In some families, the prospective student may have to deal with a background that is at best neutral towards the prospect of higher study and in some cases against. The opportunity to study at home and access to computers may be equally limited.

Individuals may be more inclined to live at home and to maintain existing social and community links rather than participating in the different range of social experiences available when living away from home as a 'traditional' undergraduate. The student lifestyle which figures so prominently in the marketing material of many universities may not in itself contain many attractions and indeed may have connotations of elitism and social exclusion. The student's expectation of what constitutes the 'higher education experience' may be very different. Combining study with part time work may not be driven only by economic necessity. Part time employment, often begun before embarking on higher level study may form part of a planned career path.

Alongside a background in which family support may be less consistent, students studying higher education courses in a further education college may come from relatively low-achieving schools. As a consequence, they may under-rate their own academic ability and may not have achieved their full potential whilst at school. Hence, they may feel, however erroneously, that they cannot meet the entrance criteria for higher education courses, or that they lack the intellectual capacity to meet the demands of higher-level study. Lack of contact with current undergraduates or those with recent experience of higher education may compound the problem.

Perhaps in contrast with a more traditional view of higher education, interest in a job or career may be a key motivator, with the main incentive to study being perceived better job prospects or earnings. This may not be the same phenomenon as the 'graduate premium' as many of the vocational areas chosen will been in less well-developed sectors of the economy or those with a history of rewarding employees less well, for example in the public sector or service industries. This may increase in importance as employers recognise the value of higher-level skills and demand them from those seeking supervisory or technical posts. In some cases, higher-level qualifications are seen to offer better job security or the prospect of self employment at a later stage in their career.

Students may be more likely to require breaks in study for economic or personal reasons as for some the arrangements made to facilitate study in the first place prove unreliable. Modular or credit accumulation systems may have a direct appeal, with the additional benefit that reluctant or fragile learners are given reassurance and credit for achievement as they progress.

From 2006, with the introduction of increased levels of fees, widening participation students may be more debt-averse than their contemporaries and thus inclined to study close to home. There is also the clear risk that for some, the combination of fees and debt may be such a disincentive that potential students from lower socio-economic groups will be so discouraged as to decide against higher education, certainly as full-time students.

Other issues arise for those students who have followed vocational pathways, either in an FE college or as part of a work-based apprenticeship. Colleges report increasing numbers of vocational Level 3 FE students expressing interest in college-based HE provision. In most cases such learners would not consider study at a university and may in any event experience difficulty in obtaining full credit for the vocational qualifications they have worked hard to achieve.

The reasons cited for choosing a further education college for higher study include familiarity with staff and institution, similar course structures and assessment methodologies, smaller teaching groups and more individual support. Such learners may be more interested in a two year Foundation Degree programme than a standard three year honours degree, although success on the former may raise confidence and encourage progression.

Finally, the role of further education colleges in providing for adult learners should not be ignored. Many mature students, particularly those with family responsibilities, will not be able to study at any distance from home. A more local further education college may be the only alternative. Additionally, many learners from this group will tend to make final decisions about participation rather late in the day, as they need certainty on matters such as child care, financial security and even transport arrangements. This in turn may make them more likely to study at a place near to home, in many cases the further education college in which they have studied. In the same way, some colleges are key providers of HE for members of ethnic or religious groups for whom study away from home is not an option.

What is offered?

As with the characteristics of the students studying higher education in further education colleges, it can be misleading to generalise about the curriculum offer available in colleges. Most college provision is in vocational subject areas. As indicated above, some of this is highly specialised. Increasingly, colleges are in dialogue with validating universities about the issues surrounding validation of provision of which the university has no direct experience. For example, some universities have had difficulty in responding to requests to validate courses such as complementary therapies, which are increasingly popular amongst FE students but in which the university may have no expertise or provision of its own. If students studying in subject areas with no established tradition of progression to higher levels of study are to be encouraged to go to a higher level clear progression routes are essential. The brokerage arrangements supported by Foundation Degree Forward may be one response to this.

FE colleges generally teach students in smaller classes and for more hours per week, in line with the FE model. This is due, in part, to the recruitment position many colleges face against increasing competition from other providers both in the HE sector and from colleges themselves. Individual student support is also considered to be more readily available. Students progressing from an FE context may expect such support and may need additional time and specific support to become independent learners in HE. For vocational learners, there may be a need for additional tutorial support to cope with different assessment methods.

Finally, part-time courses occupy a more central role for most colleges. The recently announced key role for colleges in the government's Skills Strategy raises obvious questions about part-time progression routes and the development of credible and accessible alternatives for work-based learners. The close links with local employers enjoyed by FE colleges will have advantages in identifying and developing new means of delivery best suited to part-time students.

Colleges, universities and the funding councils

As Further Education Corporations ('FECs'), colleges have a primary relationship with the Learning and Skills Council for both the funding and planning of provision. Although that body funds some higher-level work, in the form of 'non-prescribed higher education', the key priorities of provision for 16–18 year olds and adults without a first Level 2 qualification or with basic skills needs take precedence. Most colleges fund and plan their higher education offer in partnership with an HEI. In the absence of a national framework for such relationships, there is little consistency in approach or content. Even Mixed Economy Colleges, with their significant proportion of directly funded higher education, usually find themselves in an indirectly funded franchised provision for at least some of what they offer.

Against this background of a multiplicity of approaches, some college–university relationships have foundered over issues such as the division of funding, validation arrangements and the amount of support and in some cases intervention from the sponsoring HEI. In some cases there have been additional complications caused by the competitive nature of the market for higher education, with colleges and universities seeking to attract the same students to similar courses.

The introduction of Access Agreements from 2006 will raise additional issues. Indirectly funded colleges will be obliged to implement the Access arrangements adopted by their partner university. In cases where colleges have more than one indirectly funded relationship, prospective students will be faced with differing terms and benefits. Directly funded colleges will have an Access Agreement of their own. Although market forces may operate in favour of students from the widening-participation group, there is a significant risk that complex arrangements making comparison between providers difficult will be a disincentive for some potential students.

Colleges and the new higher education

As indicated above, colleges are in a process of transition, both in terms of their further education offer and as providers of higher education. Uncertainty about the impact of higher fees, plus the new demands being placed on partnerships with universities as funding or validation partners create difficulties for all aspects of planning. Discussions have indicated several key factors which, it is believed, will determine success both for colleges and for initiatives to widen participation more generally.

Many of the students needed to meet both government targets and the expectations of funders and institutions may not initially place a high priority on the value of higher-level study. Given the already intensive marketing of higher education providers, it seems likely that significant increases in student numbers will only be achieved from this group if a number of key criteria are met.

Students will demand clear information on courses and the financial implications of study. There is seen to be a real risk that students from the widening-participation group will be deterred by any uncertainty about eligibility for bursaries or the impact of increased fees and costs of study. There are clear implications for institutions and advisers for the way in which they explain the various incentives on offer. The more complicated the message and the more exceptions and qualifications it contains, the less likely students are to respond.

'Fragile' students (i.e. those both least likely to participate and most likely to drop out) may require transition mentoring, to guide and support them in the early months of higher-level study, when they are most at risk. At least to begin with, the level of support required will be on a similar scale to that offered by the students' college. Indeed, there is emerging evidence that continuity of support can have real advantages. Several colleges and their university partners are looking at ways in which college staff can be available to work with students during the early weeks of their higher level course to provide guidance and reassurance. In the same spirit, lecturers from the university are becoming involved with second year FE programmes and in some cases final year foundation degree students, to ensure that progression pathways are clear and that individual students are familiar not only with the demands of their course but also the academic staff likely to be working with them.

Curriculum models will have to be accessible and preferably reflect the need to recognise and reward achievement as it happens. Students from an FE college accustomed to more practical skills-based assessment will need regular monitoring of progress. Coupled with increased economic mobility and volatile labour markets, this can be expected to enhance the appeal of modular or credit-bearing courses. Study breaks for family or financial reasons may become an essential component of course design.

In addition, widening-participation students will expect to be able to follow the vocational curriculum pathways they have chosen in the FE college. Such provision will need to be relevant to employer needs and potentially contain a different balance of skills and knowledge compared with more traditional degree pathways. As indicated above, more traditional forms of academic assessment such as the essay may be challenged for their relevance not to academic study but to the world of work.

Institutions will be expected to recognise and, where possible, accredit experience gained in the workplace.

Students from the widening-participation groups may have different expectations of higher-level study, which do not reflect traditional academic or institutional values. Study may be seen more as a 'job', or a means to an end, rather than as an activity of value purely in its own right. Institutions can expect students to become even more demanding in terms of the quality of their experience and the value of the outcome as the new market for higher education begins to take effect. Given the planned increase in the number of citizens with higher education qualifications, and the new areas in which qualifications are becoming available, institutions may not be able to rely on the graduate premium and future high earnings as a reason for participation. Issues such as job security or maintenance of employment may be of equal importance.

Finally, although much Foundation Degree development has been predicated on the necessity for direct progression pathways to final honours degrees, many learners and colleges would like to see the Foundation Degree recognised as a qualification in its own right. In many technical and professional areas of study (e.g. construction and the built environment) academic qualifications are seen to have value only in so far as they gain exemption from the requirements of the professional bodies important in that field. Foundation Degrees in appropriate disciplines may have to satisfy the demands of these bodies if they are to attract the learners currently studying and gaining exemption via Higher National qualifications or by preparing for the assessments devised by the professions themselves.

Conclusion

Despite the best efforts of universities and pressure groups over many years to widen participation, there are still individuals and groups for whom higher education is an unrealised dream. Colleges can provide for many of them. However, they cannot do it alone. Universities are vital partners in validation and maintenance of standards. Constructive dialogue should answer many of the seemingly insoluble problems which face us now. These include developing systems to accredit work-based experience, more flexible credit-based provision, which facilitates transfer between institutions, and clear, relevant progression routes. Equally, colleges have to be realistic about what is within their capabilities and what can best be done either with close HEI support or by the HEI itself. Many colleges will be able to offer new qualifications such as Foundation Degrees, but may struggle with the resource and academic demands of offering final honours provision. Whatever the precise nature and details of the relationship, close partnerships with universities will be essential to encourage progression.

Colleges also have a part to play in persuading both employers and those in employment to recognise the benefits of higher-level skills. Some of the experience gained in working with employers to deliver the FE curriculum will be of direct relevance and vital in ensuring a continuity of offer.

Whatever the shape of higher education post 2006, colleges will continue to have a vital role to play as part of their local community, as active partners with other institutions and as part of a national framework engaging learners hitherto under-represented.

5

Are Foundation Degrees designed for widening participation? 'Is the Foundation Degree a turtle or a fruit fly?'

Derek Longhurst

Introduction

In their penetrating analysis of New Labour higher education policy since 2001 Watson and Bowden (2005) develop the conceit of the turtle, representing long-term strategic policies that are consistently supported and based upon research and evidence, and the fruit fly, representing short-term 'initiatives' that are here-today-and-gone-tomorrow. This chapter is an exploration of their question in relation to the potential of Foundation Degrees for widening participation.

Context and policy

In September 1999 the Prime Minister set a target of 50 per cent entry to higher education for the age range 18–30. This target has been subject to subsequent amendments, referring to 'experience' of higher education, for instance, in order to allow for more flexible interpretations of what the target might mean in practice. It may be argued with some justice that this prime ministerial target, subsequently endorsed within New Labour's Election Manifesto in 2001, was no more profound than recognition that higher education participation rates in England lag behind those of N. Ireland, Wales and Scotland where 50 per cent participation rates have already been achieved. In each case, of course, there are specific contextual conditions that have contributed to such participation rates. In Scotland, for instance, the achievement of a participation rate of 50 per cent is heavily dependent upon the expansion of Higher National qualifications in the FE sector.

Building upon the analysis of Sir Ron Dearing's Committee of Inquiry into higher education (1997), the (then) Secretary of State for Education, David Blunkett, announced the creation of the new Foundation Degree qualification in his speech 'Modernising higher education: meeting the global challenge' delivered at the University of Greenwich in February 2000. The title itself signals the characteristic New Labour themes of 'modernisation' of a public sector service, the knowledge economy and global competition. There were two policy initiatives that were to be developed out of these preoccupations. One was the 'e-university'; the other is the Foundation Degree.

It is worth reviewing the original conceptualisation of the Foundation Degree in some detail in order to draw out the threads in the argument underpinning the first new higher education qualification since the 1970s:

> If we are to become a leading knowledge based economy we must create new routes into higher education and new forms of provision. Our historic skills deficit lies in people with intermediate skills – including highly-qualified technicians. We have to develop new higher education opportunities at this level, orientated strongly to the employability skills, specialist knowledge and broad understanding needed in the new economy. We therefore intend to create new two year Foundation Degrees to help meet our objective that half of all young people benefit from higher education by the age of 30. Last year some 80,000 students with two or more A Levels, or the vocational equivalent, did not enter higher education directly. That's more than one in three of those who gained qualifications at this standard. (Blunkett, 2000)

It is clear, therefore, that the government's participation target did play a role in originating the Foundation Degree. But the speech signals equally that this cannot be achieved by 'more of the same' and that the qualification should be seen as a 'new form' of higher education. Blunkett seems to be addressing the same kind of issues that have subsequently underpinned the development of Lifelong Learning Networks in that there is a concern that more people have the capacity to benefit from higher education than are currently accessing it. The weakness, of course, is that which is endemic in the target in the first place: its commitment to a particular age range. In all likelihood this is a consequence of a narrow focus upon the needs of the economy, underpinned by research projections of a significant expansion of employment opportunities at the associate professional and technical levels by 2010.

The other significant theme underpinning the speech is the traditional dichotomy between vocational and academic education. From the beginning the Foundation Degree is seen as hybrid:

The Foundation Degree will offer a new vocationally-focused route into higher education. It will be academically rigorous and will provide an accessible and flexible building block for lifelong learning and future career success, drawing together further and higher education and the world of work. It will be designed to be highly valued in the labour market and appeal to a wide range of students, including the most able....For students wishing to continue their learning, there will be the opportunity to progress to an honours degree with only one-and-a-third extra years of study.

This attempt to create a positive identity for the new qualification with distinctive characteristics would, of course, come up against the weight of scepticism within the academic community at large. It can be seen, for instance, in Alison Wolf's virtual dismissal of the Foundation Degree as yet another government initiative doomed to failure. Why would 'successful' students, employers or, indeed, anyone else take them seriously as 'anything but second best'? Arguably, in her desire to interrogate the 'government's vocational rhetoric' she fails to explore how the Foundation Degree concept offers significant challenges to institutions that could lead to potential benefits for students. Instead, she reverts to the usual academic tropes, projecting that the Foundation Degree will be relevant only for 'the less academically qualified'. (Wolf, 2002: 183–4) This draws upon the embedded notion of intermediate qualifications as 'sub-degree' or a 'failed academic route.'

It is obviously incumbent upon higher education institutions that they question government policy and unpick its rhetoric. Equally, however, there is a responsibility across the sector to confront its own failures, limitations and values and to take up adventurous and creative ideas whatever their origin. Despite the expansion of higher education over the last decade, for instance, higher education has not enhanced the participation of people from Social Classes IV and V. There is an embedded mindset that values 'academic' education above 'vocational training'. It is at least arguable that many widening participation strategies have focused around the needs and structures of institutions at least as much or more than the needs of learners.

It is the argument of this chapter that Foundation Degrees have the potential to address all of these issues.

Foundation Degrees: design theory

The distinctive characteristics of the new qualification were developed in a HEFCE Prospectus (HEFCE, 2000). While this sought to draw out the distinctive identity of the new qualification, many in higher education struggled to understand the substantial difference between the Foundation Degree and other intermediate qualifications such as the HND. Some interpretations drew the conclusion that the key distinction lay in the integration of work-based learning into the programme of study and that, therefore, the Foundation Degree could only be developed fully in a 'part-time' mode. Others saw the full-time mode as essential to their own business needs and recruitment markets.

This uncertainty around the practice of designing and developing the new qualification led HEFCE to commission the Quality Assurance Agency to undertake a Foundation Degree review during 2003. The Agency also developed a *Foundation Degree Qualification Benchmark (Final Draft)* published in October 2002. This was defined as a final draft as it would be revised in relation to the review of practice to be undertaken through scrutiny of 34 Foundation Degrees; it was subsequently published in its final form during November 2004 (QAA, 2004). It is worth dwelling on this document as it is now widely accepted as the key reference point for the design and development of a Foundation Degree.

The qualification benchmark defines the Foundation Degree as follows:

> *The distinctiveness of Foundation Degrees depends upon the* integration *of the following characteristics: employer involvement; accessibility; articulation and progression; flexibility; and partnership. While none of these attributes is unique to Foundation Degrees, their clear and planned integration within a single award, underpinned by work-based learning, makes the award very distinctive.* (Para. 24; emphasis added)

This makes it clear that employer engagement in the design and development of Foundation Degrees is absolutely fundamental to practice. Where possible, too, institutions should work with employers to involve them in aspects of delivery and assessment. Commonly, this focuses around the development and *integration* of work-based learning into the programme of study. There have been numerous debates about the definition of work-based learning and its practice, especially in relation to different sectors, but the essential point here is that the objective for Foundation Degrees is to establish a different order of engagement with both employers and the workplace. Generally, this is seen as an attempt to address the perennial complaint by employers that higher education does not deliver a trained workforce ready for the 'world of work'. There are, however, other more potentially innovative outcomes to be derived out of a serious engagement with work-based learning.

One of these is pedagogic and is registered in the QAA Benchmark:

> *Authentic and innovative work-based learning is an integral part of Foundation Degrees and their design. It enables learners to take on appropriate role(s) within the workplace, giving them the opportunity to learn and apply the skills and knowledge they have acquired as an integrated element of the programme. It involves the development of higher-level learning within both the institution and the workplace. It should be a two-way process…Work-based learning requires the identification and achievement of defined and related learning outcomes.*

This suggests a planned interaction between learning environments that would shape both pedagogy and curriculum content. Thus, one challenge of Foundation Degrees is to develop a curriculum that is *equally* informed by National Occupational Standards as by the more widely 'accepted' subject benchmarks defined by academic communities. This supports the potential of the qualification to attract into higher education people for whom traditional full-time academic programmes are either unattractive, or financially problematic, or both.

The emphasis on innovation in relation to the Foundation Degree is an important one. Clearly, it is in no one's interest, least of all that of students, if the qualification is seen as 'second best' for 'less academically able students' in Alison Wolf's terms. Thus, the qualification benchmark clearly seeks to embody a required level of achievement that is challenging and clearly located at the intermediate level of the Framework for Higher Education Qualifications. This is spelt out in detail against the Level Descriptor Learning Outcomes that provision is required to meet. Students will be required to demonstrate, for instance: 'knowledge and critical understanding' of the principles informing their field of study; 'ability to apply underlying concepts and principles outside the context in which they were first studied'; ability to 'evaluate critically' different methodological approaches; 'an understanding of the limits of their knowledge.' Work-based learning is integral to these learning outcomes. Consequently there is a clear emphasis on capacities for lifelong learning in the Foundation Degree.

The remaining core characteristics of the Foundation Degree qualification clearly manifest the widening-participation agenda: they are accessibility, partnership, progression and flexibility. Largely, the first three of these have been seen as related to the collaboration of HEIs and FECs in the design, development and delivery of Foundation Degrees. In general, FECs provide more supportive environments that are attractive and more accessible for some students; there are also traditions of collaboration between local and regional employers and training programmes offered by FECs and these could be built upon to establish Foundation Degrees. Generally, the role of universities is to be accountable for validation and quality assurance; setting and moderating standards of achievement is clearly central to this activity.

Deriving out of the Secretary of State's formulation there has always been a requirement that the validating university should provide an *option* for students of progression to an appropriate honours degree. There have been debates around this issue, including perspectives that suggest such progression may undermine the identity of the Foundation Degree as a qualification in its own right. Validating institutions may experience difficulty in providing coherent progression routes for Foundation Degree students and may, therefore, shape the qualification to 'fit' more traditional qualifications. On the other hand, the provision of progression routes provides some motivation for validating universities to 'buy in' to the qualification and to ensure that it is not perceived as 'second best'. The overwhelming argument must surely be that the requirement provides opportunities for those students who may wish to make use of the option because they have discovered something about themselves and gained in confidence through the experience of the Foundation Degree.

Finally, there is an explicit requirement that institutions develop flexibility in their provision of Foundation Degrees. There are a number of dimensions to this core characteristic and all of them have implications in relation to the potential for widening participation. The integration of work-based learning into Foundation Degrees carries with it the impetus to develop blended learning approaches, distance learning materials and technology-assisted learning support. Additionally, design teams need to introduce learning contracts and Personal Development Planning (PDP) into their delivery modes. Consequently, Foundation Degrees have often been developed to offer delivery around the lives and commitments of learners rather than 'fitting them in' to existing institutional structures and traditions of delivery. This also has an impact upon definitions of full-time and part-time modes. All too often institutions have simply seen the part-time mode as doing a full-time programme over a longer period of time. The Foundation Degree encourages a more radical approach to the part-time mode in positive ways, again in relation to the requirements of part-time learners and the patterns of their commitments.

Foundation Degrees: design in practice

So, how, then, are Foundation Degrees doing since their first year of operation in 2001–2002?

In terms of overall growth the current picture is represented in Figure 1.

Some impetus has been provided by the HEFCE Additional Student Numbers process in support of Foundation Degrees, but research conducted by 'Foundation Degree Forward' in consultation with providing institutions suggests that there are currently 1390 FDs in operation nationally with major growth in the north-west and south-west regions particularly. An additional 748 programmes are planned for introduction in 2005–2006.

It is fairly clear that provision has initially been driven by public sector workforce development where there is also student demand in significant numbers, but there is also large scale development in business,

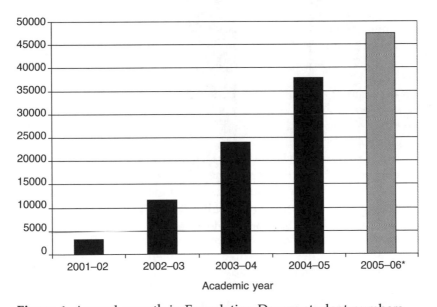

Figure 1. Annual growth in Foundation Degree student numbers.

Note: The figure given for 2005–06 is a prediction based on trends in annual growth over the preceding four- year period

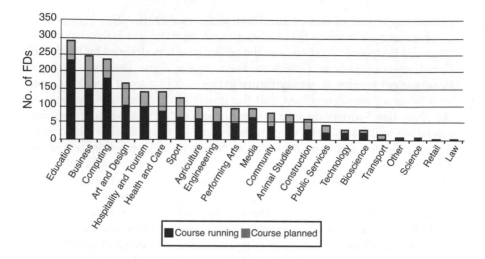

Figure 2. Foundation Degrees by subject area in 2004–05.

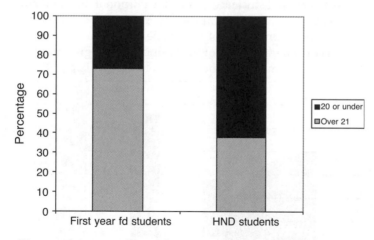

Figure 3. Age profile of first year Foundation Degree students in 2003–04: Data source: HESA press release 86

computing, creative and cultural industries (see Figure 2).

There is no evidence that development, to date, has been driven by Regional Economic Strategies or the priority sectors defined by Regional Development Agencies. There are encouraging signs, however, at least in some regions that this may figure in the next phases of development.

It is sometimes suggested that the growth in Foundation Degrees is simply related to the decline in the market for HNs and that they are attracting only students who would have entered higher education anyway. There are a number of factors that suggest this is overly simplistic. In part, the sectors in which there has been most growth has led to some age and gender differences in terms of student profile (Figures 3 and 4).

HESA data for 2003–04 indicate that 73 per cent of first year Foundation Degree students were defined as mature, while 62 per cent of HND students were aged 20 or under. There is a significant difference, however, between full-time and part-time modes of Foundation Degrees in terms of gender (Figure 5).

The significance of this profile of part-time mature women students is that it will have, in common with other higher education qualifications attracting comparable students, an impact upon retention and completion data. Again, it is clearly simplistic to relate withdrawal rates to quality of provision as some kind of inevitable equation.

Accessibility is a core characteristic of the Foundation Degree and this has been seen largely in terms of collaboration between HEIs and FECs.

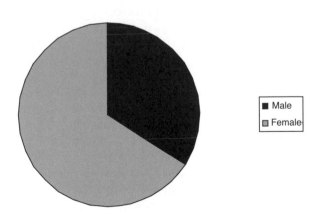

Figure 4. Gender profile of first year Foundation Degree students in 2003–04: Data source: HESA press release 86.

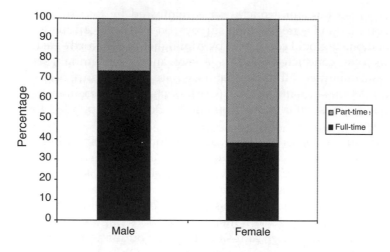

Figure 5: Gender of first year Foundation Degree students by mode of study in 2003–04: Source: Report of a survey to follow up Foundation Degree reviews carried out in 2002-03 (QAA, 2005).

Collaborative provision frequently receives a bad press, with issues of costs and quality attracting headlines. There is emerging evidence that the Foundation Degree is providing a focus for the development of more coherent and strategic partnerships. As there will be around 1682 Foundation Degrees running in FE colleges in 2005–2006, constituting 79 per cent of Foundation Degree programmes, this suggests that such partnerships between colleges and their validating institutions are being forged. The QAA Review conducted during 2005 has provided further evidence that this is so. Indeed, the QAA data collated for the review process indicate a 72 per cent increase in delivery sites for Foundation Degrees between 2002 and 2004.

In 2005 the Quality Assurance Agency published its follow-up survey of the Foundation Degrees reviewed in 2003. This report concludes that 'FDs are successful in providing a new award at intermediate level...which links and integrates work-based learning (WBL) and academic studies.' More particularly, the report comments that:

> *The introduction of the FD award has given providers new opportunities to offer higher education (HE) programmes to a range of sectors. There is some evidence, particularly from students, that the FD is attracting students who had not previously considered entering HE.*

The evidence to support this conclusion is reinforced by two further substantial Foundation Degree student surveys, one national conducted by AGCAS and one regional conducted by Aimhigher in the North-East. The AGCAS survey, conducted by Chris Jackson and Eddie Tunnah, set out to provide an analysis of the information, advice and guidance needs of Foundation Degree students. In total, 639 students in 19 different institutions studying almost 50 different Foundation Degrees responded to the questionnaire.

The AGCAS survey indicates that 'a high proportion of respondents had little experience of HE within their family. Only around one in five (21 per cent) said one of their parents had a degree or HND; less than one-third (31 per cent) a sibling; and only just over one-third (35 per cent) another relative.' (Jackson and Tunnah, 2005: 5). Only 18 per cent of students had applied for their Foundation Degree during clearing admissions and 73 per cent said that the Foundation Degree was their first choice to enhance career prospects. Only 22 per cent had wanted to do an honours degree, a more common motivation amongst younger full-time Foundation Degree students. It is worth noting that 6 per cent of students already had a degree or higher qualification already.

The Aimhigher North East survey, *Learner Experience of Foundation Degrees in the North East of England: Access, Support and Progression* was conducted by Richard Dodgson and Helen Whitham. Where the AGCAS survey had some imbalance towards full-time provision, the Aimhigher survey had a more evenly balanced split between full-time and part-time respondents (537). In this case only 11.2 per cent of students had parents with previous experience of higher education. There would seem to be a *prima facie* case, therefore, to support the view that Foundation Degrees are making a contribution to widening participation and attracting people to 'first-time entry' into higher education.

But are they being recruited to 'second-best' programmes? The QAA survey concludes that:

> The survey suggests that learning and teaching continue to be areas of strength. Students experience a variety of teaching methods and are encouraged to develop higher level skills such as critical evaluation and analysis.... The use of virtual learning environments continues to increase and develop. Students value the ability to access programme materials at any time.

This broad conclusion is supported by the student surveys where only about 5–8 per cent of respondents indicated that their Foundation Degree is not serving their needs or is a 'not very good' learning experience.

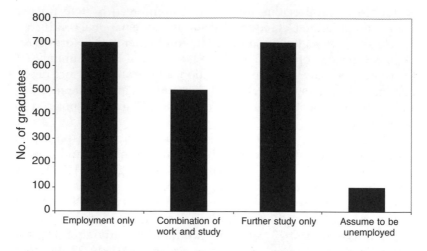

Figure 6: First destination of Foundation Degree graduates (2003–04): Data source: HESA press release 89.

This needs to be taken into account when it comes to any assessment of retention rates in Foundation Degrees. Mature, part-time learners need strong systems of support but they will often withdraw from Foundation Degrees for reasons other than the quality of this provision. It is useful, then, to examine the trends in progression amongst the first Foundation Degree graduates (see Figure 6).

Conclusion

Returning to where we began: In *The turtle and the fruit fly: New Labour and UK higher education, 2001–2005*, David Watson and Rachel Bowden reach the:

> *...brutal conclusion that we have higher education policy-making where 'evidence' only counts if it will fit the narrative; in fact we are in the realm of 'non-evidence based policy'...*

Amongst other manifestations of this trend in government policy-making, the evidence suggests:

> *That foundation degrees will fail if they are heavily promoted as a system-wide supply-side recipe for growth – what could have been a really imaginative, high quality new venture...will collapse under the weight of expectation and likely 'lowest common denominator' development....*

The irony here is that there is evidence that this is a view that would be shared by government policy-makers! One of the consistent themes in the skills strategies, represented in the two White Papers published in July 2003 and March 2005, has been employer engagement in educational provision. There are those, like Alison Wolf, who may regard much of this as government rhetoric and refer to the track record of employers in not supporting NVQs. Nevertheless, there has been a consistent focus on 'demand-driven' Foundation Degrees related to employer-defined skills deficits and informed by Sector Skills Council frameworks.

Thus, institutions are urged to undertake detailed market analysis, consult with employers and employer organisations and regional economic strategies in order to develop Foundation Degrees that are responsive to demand rather than being 'supply-driven' in the way that is more common in other forms of higher education. There are a number of tensions here, including matching employee/student demand with employer demand. There have been attempts to bind such considerations into the ASN (Additional Student Numbers) bidding process in 2004 and 2005, which otherwise have been introduced to create the context for Foundation Degree development across the further and higher education sector.

One of the brakes upon expansion of higher education is the cost to the treasury of student support. Consequently, the issue of employer engagement needs to be seen in the overall context of a 'market' in higher education with the introduction of variable fees. One potential development around Foundation Degrees is the construction of a context that promotes co-financing of the qualification involving employers, students and public funding.

Again, this needs to be understood in terms of the possibilities for widening participation in that 'demand-driven' Foundation Degrees challenge institutional practices and structures to design programmes that are 'custom-built' and not off the shelf. Thus, in answering the question posed at the head of this chapter the argument has been that higher education institutions need to seize the opportunities offered by the Foundation Degree, despite their costs, and to ensure that they are 'imaginative and high quality ventures' as described above. This will take time. Like other forms of educational provision, Foundation Degrees are complex to design and we should not submit them to requirements or judgments that are not applied to other new programmes. It is worth noting the comment of the QAA survey of the Foundation Degrees reviewed in 2003:

Providers have learnt from their early FD programmes and have taken steps to enhance the provision. They have also taken forward this learning in the development of other FDs. (Report of a survey to follow up Foundation Degree reviews carried out in 2002-2003: 1)

Institutions should find creative ways of articulating the qualification in ways that meet the needs of learners and their existing or potential employers. In so doing they will be confronting the issues posed by Geoff Layer in his Preface to *Closing the equity gap: The impact of widening participation strategies in the UK and the USA* (Layer, 2005):

> *The challenge is to change the curriculum, the environment and the culture so that it meets the needs of learners, not to change the learner so that they meet the needs of the university.*

References

Blunkett, D (2000) Speech at University of Greenwich, 15 February 2000, DfES, Press Notice 2000/0064, London: DfES.

DfES (Department for Education and Skills) (2005) *Skills: Getting on in business, getting on at work,* London: The Stationery Office.

Dodgson, R and Whitham, H (2005) *Learner Experience of Foundation Degrees in the North east of England: Access, Support and Progression,* Sunderland: Aimhigher North East.

Duke, C (2005) *The Tertiary Moment: What road to inclusive higher education?* Leicester: NIACE.

Gallacher, J and Osborne, M (2005) *A Contested Landscape: International perspectives on diversity in mass higher education,* Leicester: NIACE.

HEFCE (Higher Education Funding Council for England) (2000) *Foundation Degree Prospectus,* Bristol: HEFCE.

Jackson, C and Tunnah, E (2005) *The Information, Advice and Guidance Needs of Foundation Degree Students – report of an AGCAS survey.* Sheffield: AGCAS.

Layer, G (2005) *Closing the equity gap?* Leicester: NIACE.

NCIHE (National Committee of Inquiry into Higher Education) (1997) *Higher Education in the Learning Society (the Dearing Report),* London: HMSO.

QAA (Quality Assurance Agency for Higher Education) (2002) *Foundation Degree Qualification Benchmark (Final Draft),* Gloucester: QAA.

QAA (Quality Assurance Agency for Higher Education) (2004) *Foundation Degree Qualification Benchmark,* Gloucester: QAA.

QAA (Quality Assurance Agency for Higher Education) (2005) *Report of a Survey to Follow Up Foundation Degree Reviews Carried out in 2002–04,* Gloucester: QAA.

Watson, D and Bowden, R (2005) *The Turtle and the Fruit Fly: New Labour and UK higher education 2001–2005.* University of Brighton Education Research Centre Occasional Paper.

Wolf, A (2002) *Does Education Matter? Myths about Education and Economic Growth.* London: Penguin.

Sources of further information

Lifelong Learning Networks: HEFCE Website www.hefce.ac.uk/widen/lln/

6

What About the Workers? Workplace Learning and widening participation

Bob Fryer

Some puzzles and paradoxes

When it comes to discussions about access to learning or to considerations of widening participation, the issue of workplace learning raises many paradoxes and puzzles. On the one hand, and at the most banal level, it has now become something of a truism simply to assert that the workplace is a major locale for adult learning, maybe even constituting the principal place for learning or for creating learning opportunities for many adults. As Alan Felstead and his colleagues remark, in their commentary on the 2004 Learning at Work Survey, 'working provides the most important source of learning once in a job. In other words, the most effective classroom is often the workplace itself'. (Felstead *et al*, 2005, Executive Summary)

Yet, on the other hand, much of the literature and the policy debates, in the UK at least, about widening access, participation in learning, achievement and progression still focuses mainly upon evidence drawn from traditional and formal educational settings in schools, further education colleges and higher education. What is more, there is still much better and more routine information readily available and much more systematic and reliable data provided about the social composition and achievements (or lack of them) of learners in formal institutions of education than there is about learning in the world of work. (However, there are increasingly some useful data about workplace learning which deserve closer attention than they are usually given, as we shall see.) Why is this so, especially if there is some truth in the claims about the centrality of learning, or for the potential for learning, *at, for, in* or *through* work?

Before exploring this paradox further, it is worth briefly mentioning a group of related puzzles and apparent contradictions. First, if workplace learning really is so important, or can at least be said to be *increasingly* important, why are the pedagogies and androgies of genuinely work-based learning so relatively underdeveloped and so lacking in robust academic scrutiny and review, and why are the special skills of fostering successful learning through work so little recognised? Second, what explains the fact that far more attention has been given to developing a complex variety of funding and business models for financing effective education in formal education settings and to putting them on legal or quasi-legal footing than has been given to creating systematic ways of paying for and resourcing workplace learning?

Despite some small and welcome elements of progress recently, funding for learning at, for, in or through work in the UK, especially the provision of public funding or the clarification of individuals' entitlements, is still piecemeal, fragmented, inconsistent, largely voluntaristic and mostly inadequate. Finally, given that emphasising the value of workplace learning and campaigning for it have very long pedigrees in the UK and elsewhere, for example, in trade union circles – some of this long pre-dating the public provision of universal and compulsory primary and secondary education, let alone the growth of further and higher education – what explains this continuing relative neglect?

Varieties of workplace learning

The best way to seek answers to these puzzles and paradoxes, or at least understand them better, is to examine current arguments, policies and practices in relation to workplace learning. Before doing so, it is worth recognising, first, that the broad term 'workplace learning' is something of an omnibus category and there is no agreement or clarity about its precise meaning. At a minimum, it embraces a whole variety of learning forms and practices, ranging from provision and activity that is highly *formal and structured* to that which is *informal, non-formal* and even *'tacit'*. Some of this learning will be work-*related*, some will be work-*oriented*, some will be *informed* or shaped by work and some will be *inherent* in the very social and technical processes of work. Workplace learning occurs both *on the job* and *off*; both *at* work and *away* from the immediate work-site. Some elements of workplace learning will be *embedded* in jobs or in workplace cultures or communities of one kind or another, some will be almost wholly *experiential* and some will be deliberately generated, or *constructed*, almost entirely out of the work situation itself and be properly thought of as work-*based*. Some workplace learning might lead to *qualifications* or to *credits* and some will, no doubt, be undertaken with the express purpose of meeting the requirements of a given *voca-*

tion or *profession,* and much may not. Some workplace learning will be *explicit, systematic and subject to rigorous quality checks,* and some will not. Similarly, some of this learning will be *recognised,* legitimated and even rewarded by managers, or by educationalists, or by fellow workers or by some communities of practice.

Finally, some of this workplace learning may be frowned upon, be regarded as *disruptive* or may attract *sanctions or disciplinary action* by some parties, especially those in authority. Only the naïve or the permanently optimistic believe that all learning and all forms of learning can be regarded as positive experiences by all those affected by it. So, workplace learning cannot be assumed always to serve a supposedly common set of interests or result in desired outcomes that are shared and equally valued by all parties. There is, after all, a long and well-documented history of workers using workplace learning and their intimate knowledge and understanding of work processes and practices to defend their own interests. In these instances, workers' learning, and the practices and knowledge based on it, can act as a form of resistance to managerial initiatives, or serve to assert their own forms of counter-control over such things as ways of working, management discretion, payment systems, productivity and efficiency drives, and organisational change. There are, too, many examples of workers using their own understanding and learning to resist what they have seen as employers' concerted attempts to 'de-skill' their work, or appropriate the essence of their skills into technology or other new ways of working. Some learning may be resisted, or at least resented, by workers who see it as a managerial, or government-inspired, unwelcome imposition.

All of these distinctions and caveats are important and, strictly speaking, an appreciation of them should inform any full and rigorous consideration of workplace learning (which is seldom the case). Indeed, some aspects of the puzzles and paradoxes already mentioned here derive precisely from a failure to differentiate between different kinds of workplace learning and their implications for employment on the one hand or for debates about learning, including issues of access and participation, on the other. However, for our immediate purposes at this stage, it is enough to emphasise that the range, types and forms of learning at work are at least as varied as those found in formal educational settings, if not more so, as, indeed, are the various meanings and interpretations given to key terms in the debate, such as 'learning', 'participation' and 'skill'. Workplace learning, like any other kind of learning, is not an undifferentiated, homogeneous and entirely beneficent mass, and different elements of workplace learning may be of different value to different groups, especially where there are palpable differences of interest. What is more, there is a tendency to refer to all of these different forms of workplace learning as *'work-based learning'*, which is under-standable but misleading. Genuine work-based learning, of the fully constructivist kind, is only one kind of workplace learning, albeit one that seemingly represents some of the greatest challenges to more conventional approaches to pedagogy and to the design and delivery of learning.

The current emphasis on workplace learning

Even the briefest review of UK (and other) government policies or of statements by employers confirms that there is much current emphasis upon the importance, even absolute need, for workers to be engaged in learning throughout their working lives. Employers and governments alike constantly urge that continuous updating of workers' skills and competences is essential to meet the demands of increased global competition and to match the higher levels of labour productivity found amongst firms and workers in other countries. (DfES, 2003a) They also point to the need for workplace learning to underpin the greater application of information and knowledge to work and the speeding up of routes to market through the markedly increased use of information technology. As one authority puts it:

> The shift to a post-industrial, knowledge-based economy is progressively altering the role of the traditional factors of production: labour, materials, and capital. Symbolic resources are replacing physical resources, mental exertion is replacing physical exertion, and knowledge capitalism is beginning to challenge money and all other forms of capital....It is already apparent from current trends that the organization of future work and the level of knowledge necessary to benefit from future work opportunities are going to alter dramatically and that worker skill levels are going to have to improve equally dramatically.... The firm's most valuable knowledge capital tends to reside in the brains of its key workers, and ownership of people went out with the abolition of slavery (Burton-Jones, 1999: 22)

There are many reasons for asserting the significance of workplace learning, not least the sheer amount of waking time that most adults spend at work during their lives and the importance of work for people's incomes, life chances generally, sense of themselves and well-being and integration into various work situations and communities. We all know, if only from personal experience as well as from anecdotal information, that taking up any new job requires workers to 'learn the ropes' of the new work setting, however 'skilled' they may already be. It means getting to understand the ways things are done around here, how work is organised, who is powerful, what behaviour is 'normal' or unacceptable and what are the main political and status issues in the new job. In short, it is a commonplace to accept that any work situation presents workers with a variety of cultures and sub-cultures that require learning and understanding before they can be navigated successfully. As Jay Cross (2003) puts it: 'at work we learn more in the breakroom than in the classroom. We discover how to do our jobs through informal learning – observing others, asking the person in the next cubicle, calling the help desk, trial and error, and simply working with people in the know'. Taking up even what is the apparently least-skilled job presents learning challenges, as Barbara Ehrenreich discovered in her insightful, undercover participant observation of working in some of America's lowest-paying jobs.

> *You might think that unskilled jobs would be a snap for someone who holds a PhD and whose normal line of work requires learning entirely new things every couple of weeks. Not so. The first thing I discovered is that no job, no matter how lowly, is truly 'unskilled'. Every one of the six jobs I entered into in the course of this project required concentration and most demanded that I master new terms, new tools and new skills – from placing orders on restaurant computers to wielding the backpack vacuum cleaner. None of these things came as easily to me as I would have liked. No one ever said, 'Wow, you're fast!' or 'Can you believe she just started?' Whatever the accomplishments in the rest of my life, in the low-wage work world I was a person of average ability – capable of learning the job and capable of screwing up.* (Ehrenreich, 2002: 193)

It also appropriate, if rather trite, as Field rightly remarks, to recognise that each individual human being is already a 'permanently learning subject' throughout life (Dumazadier, 1995, quoted in Field, 2000: 35). People's working lives inevitably form part of what can reasonably be called a 'learning society', not seen as some desirable but always unobtainable utopian goal, but as the living reality for all, whether acknowledged or not and, frankly, whether the individual concerned perceives it to be beneficial or not. To regard, or classify, some individuals or groups of people as 'non-learners', as for example is done explicitly in the analysis of the UK government's National Adult Learning Survey (DfES, 2003b, *passim*), can, in this sense, amount to an unintended denial of their very humanity. On the other hand, such analysis and differentiation usefully underscores the fact that some people explicitly and consciously see themselves a 'learners', identify positively with opportunities to learn and regard learning as an important part of their own self-images and lives.

By contrast, respondents who state their lack of interest in learning, or at least signal that it is not a priority in their lives and express themselves quite content with that situation, should not automatically be judged to be ill-informed, misguided or to be pitied. After all, given their prior experience of at least formal learning institutions, this might represent a purely rational and balanced response on their behalf. Perhaps, too, such different attitudes to adult learning really indicate that some respondents to the survey are more likely to share conceptions of what constitutes 'learning' with the researchers or to subscribe to an accepted or dominant notion of learning, while others do not. Either way, the data are at least suggestive, as will be seen later.

British government policies

The UK government launched its current national skills strategy in July 2003 in a White Paper entitled *21st Century Skills: Realising Our Potential* (DFES, 2003a). The strategy itself resulted from a whole series of preparatory papers, committees of inquiry and task force reports, especially the work of the National Skills Taskforce, which produced four important reports and a series of detailed research papers and statistical analyses over the years 1998–2001. Over the previous twenty years, there had also been an accumulation of an almost bewildering series of government policies and initiatives in respect of work skills. These included, notably, the creation of the Manpower Services Commission in the early 1980s, the Technical and Vocational Initiative for secondary school pupils, various youth training schemes, the introduction of National Vocational Qualifications, the merger of the government departments of Education and Employment and the establishment of a network of more than eighty local Training and Enterprise Councils and several White Papers.

The aims of the current policy were set out succinctly in *21st Century Skills*. They were to 'ensure that employers have the right skills to support the success of their businesses, and individuals have the skills they need to be both employable and personally fulfilled.' (DfES, 2003a: 11). The government's reasons for this were equally clear. The global economy had made extinct the notion of 'jobs for life', British businesses and workers were far less productive than their principal oversees competitors and the country could not expect to compete successfully on the basis of low wages. There was a particular shortage technical and 'intermediate' skills, disturbingly large numbers of adults appeared to have difficulties with so-called 'basic skills' in literacy and numeracy, and there was a need to enhance the skills of management and leadership. Too often, there was a 'mismatch' between the skills that businesses required and the programmes of learning and levels of achievement on offer from schools and further education. What this called for, said the White Paper, was a strategy based on the capacities of businesses and individuals for innovation, enterprise, better quality and adding greater value to goods and services.

Of particular interest to this chapter was the government's commitment to a strategy intended also to give emphasis to social inclusion and greater equity. As the White Paper put it:

> *This not only an economic challenge. It is just as much a social one. By increasing the skill level of all under-represented groups, we will develop an inclusive society that promotes employability for all. When people are better educated and better trained, they have the chance to earn more and use their talents to the full, both in and out of work.... We are concerned that skills and learning initiatives are not reaching all of society. We want to increase the skills levels for all under-represented groups and encourage all individuals to improve their employability. This is crucial for women workers who now constitute 44 per cent of the workforce, yet are typically locked in a narrow range of low level manual occupations and in part-time work where training opportunities are limited. It is also an issue for ethnic minorities, agency workers and other disadvantaged groups who have low skill levels.*
>
> (DfES, 2003a: 18, 20)

In this context, the White Paper drew attention to the fact that 'over 7 million adults in the workforce do not have a qualification at Level 2. Those people are more likely to lack a skills foundation for employability and lifelong learning, and are less likely to get a secure, well paid job.' (60). However, the government was at pains to underline that this was about more than just developing people's skills for work, and in doing so the White Paper hinted broadly at the government's subscription to contemporary notions about the advantages to individuals and communities of enhancing their 'social capital' as well as their skills and competences. 'Skills serve wider social purposes. For many people learning enriches their lives. They may enjoy learning for its own sake. Or it may make them better placed to give something back to their community, to help family and friends, to manage family finances better, or help their children throughout their school careers.' (60). In view of this concern with both securing greater social inclusion and the recognition of the wider virtues of learning, the White Paper indicated a commitment 'to ensure equality of access to opportunities by ensuring that public funds are focused on those most in need'. These groups included adults who are unqualified, unemployed, have disabilities, are older, obtain work through employment agencies, come from certain minority ethnic groups, or who work in part-time and low paid jobs (70).

In order to tackle these challenges, the government resolved to put in place a whole raft of reforms, initiatives and changed priorities. For the purposes of this chapter, these included a major drive to tackle the perceived problem of poor adult skills in literacy and numeracy, the reform of the Modern Apprenticeship scheme and the innovative notion of an 'entitlement' for adults to attain a first Level 2 qualification at no charge. The new strategy also included reforming qualifications, promoting Foundation Degrees, expanding opportunities for e-learning through the national network of learndirect and UK Online centres, piloting adult learning grants, increasing support for trades union 'learning representatives' and the establishment of employer-led Sector Skills Councils. All of this would be led and overseen by a National Skills Alliance, – ' a new social partnership for skills' – embracing government departments, employers, trade unions, small businesses and major delivery organisations such as UfI / learndirect.

A key addition to the strategy has been a scheme initiated by the Treasury in 2002, and carried through in partnership with the DfES, Learning and Skills Council and Regional Development Agencies in England, to establish so-called 'employer training pilots' (from 2005 transformed into the National Employers Training Programme), aimed principally at low-skilled and unqualified workers. Under this scheme, in exchange for providing targeted employees with time off for 35–70 hours to train for a first Level 2 qualification or 'basic' skills in literacy and numeracy, the government meets the costs of the training provision, pays compensation to the employer for the time taken off work, and provides free information, advice and guidance. In the first year of operating the scheme, some 14,000 people were signed up. The typical participant was female, between the ages of 25 and 35, working in a full-time, low skilled job in a small firm and left full-time education at the minimum school-leaving age. By the time of the Budget 2005, the Treasury reported that 17,000 employers were participating in the scheme and 120,000 workers were participating. Most had left school at the minimum age for leaving, half had no qualifications at all, and 70 per cent worked in firms employing fewer than 50 people.

Employers

In recent years, there has also been increasing employer and business emphasis in the UK (and elsewhere in the world) on the critical importance workforce skills and development to improve competitive advantage. There is, it is insisted, an urgent need to respond to increasing globalisation, deal with key skills' shortages and workforce skills gaps, underpin change and innovation, facilitate increased knowledge transfer and cope with the greater application of Information Technology to work. Learning is depicted as being so vital for the future success of business that serious business writers and practitioners have even championed the somewhat reified idea of the 'Learning Organisation', emphasising the importance of collective and ubiquitous learning and knowledge application in ways that infuse every aspect of an organisation's 'culture' and ethos.(Senge, 1990; Senge *et al*, 1999). There has also been much recent talk in business circles and in the publications of business school gurus of the advent of, and challenges of thriving in, the 'knowledge economy' and in the context of an accelerating worldwide 'information revolution'. They point to the urgent and the increasing significance of recognising the core value of an organisation's 'human capital' and the often hidden but vital assets of its 'intellectual capital', both of them depending crucially upon staff skills, competences and their continuous renewal and development. As one of the leading exponents of this perspective puts it:

> By 'intellectual capital' I don't mean a clutch of PhDs locked up in a lab somewhere. Nor do I mean intellectual property (such as patents and copyrights), though that is one part of intellectual capital. Intellectual capital is the sum of everything everyone in a company knows will give it a competitive edge. Unlike the assets with which business people and accountants are familiar – land, factories, equipment, cash – intellectual capital is intangible. It is the knowledge of a workforce; the training and intuition of a team of chemists who discover a billion-dollar new drug or the knowhow of workmen who come up with a thousand different ways to improve the efficiency of a factory. It is the electronic network that transports information through a company so that it can react to the market faster than its rivals. It is the collaboration – the shared learning – between a company and its customers...In a sentence: Intellectual capital is intellectual material – knowledge, information, intellectual property, experience – that can be put to use to create wealth. It is collective brainpower. (Stewart, x)

In this context, UK employers have voiced considerable criticism of the output from schools, colleges and universities. Their principal complaint is that the education system is driven far too much by the interests and priorities of the 'producers' and insufficiently geared to responding to the needs of their principal 'customers' in the market place – employers of every type and stripe. Employers' organisations, such as the Confederation of British Industry and the Institute of Directors, constantly complain that far too many young people leave school with sufficient competence in language, literacy and numeracy, and are generally unprepared for the world of work. They argue that there has been too little emphasis in education on developing what employers now see as the critical 'employability' and business skills of problem solving, team working, customer care, innovation and creativity. A Sir Digby Jones, the CBI Director General, put it recently: 'the UK is the fourth richest economy on Earth. Surely it cannot be beyond us to ensure all our young people have the basic skills they need to get on at work', (CBI, 2005).

For their part, British employers and their representative organisations have vigorously resisted any suggestion of imposing a legal obligation on employers to provide learning and development opportunities for all of their staff, or to give workers a statutory right to claim such opportunities at work, funded by the employer. To the contrary, British employers have insisted on the virtues of a 'voluntaristic' approach to workplace learning and workforce development. In this regard, increasing numbers of UK employers, especially larger companies, point out that they have sought the prestige of securing Investors in People recognition and other high-standard quality marks, with their characteristic emphasis on workforce training and development. Some have sought support their workers' development through establishing Employee Development Schemes of the kind pioneered by the Ford Company and the Transport and General Workers' Union in the celebrated EDAP scheme. Learning has increasingly been added to the collective bargaining agenda with trade unions, and even before they were given some limited statutory backing, Union Learning Representatives and shop-floor 'learning champions' were recognised by employers, providing not only an authentic voice of the workforce in discussions of learning but acting also as advocates, stimulators, informal advisers and mentors of learners and workplace learning.

Some employers have even created their own in-house so-called 'corporate universities', aimed at improving staff skills, boosting innovation and promoting what employers call 'cultural change' at work. Critics of conventional higher education's provision of workplace learning see the advent of these largely in-house initiatives as a business response to the alleged slowness, adherence to older forms of pedagogy, long duration of learning programmes and commitment to qualifications of traditional universities. For them, 'corporate' universities represent the chance of responding effectively to the pressing thrust from business for 'just-in-time' and 'just-for-you' leaning that can be accessed in easily digested and applied 'bite-sized' chunks, preferably through an e-learning medium. On the other hand, critics of such corporate initiatives and observers of a more sceptical disposition question whether they really represent a narrowing down of learning, with limitations on the scope for critical inquiry, reflection and opportunities for personal development (Jarvis, 2001).

Trade unions

As already noted, British trade unions have a long tradition of demonstrating their commitment to learning for their members. They have provided extensive training for their own full-time and lay officials, have invested in occupational and, more recently, 'basic' skills development and qualifications for members, have campaigned for improved opportunities for workers to have access to workplace learning and have added their campaigning voices to calls for reforms in general education at school and beyond to secure greater equity. Some unions have established their own residential learning centres and many have worked closely with the Workers' Educational Association to provide union education.

Since the 1980s, British unions, notably including NUPE, TGWU, USDAW, GMB, UNISON and AMICUS as well as the Trades Union Congress, have pioneered an impressive variety of 'return to learn', distance and workplace learning schemes. More recently, unions have sought to conclude workplace 'learning agreements' with employers, have developed an extensive network of lay, shop-floor, depot, and office-based 'Learning Representatives' of one kind or another and have successfully campaigned for such representatives to be given certain statutory rights at work, based on the markedly successful precedent of union Health and Safety Representatives.

The most recent development on the union front is the decision of the TUC and its affiliates, supported financially by the DfES, to establish its own Union Learning Academy, whose 'unique selling point must be that union-led collective strategies will help workers have a fairer share of learning opportunities and life chances and contribute to a higher performing economy'. (TUC, 2004: 5) The aims of the new Union Academy will include:

- to support and add value to affiliated unions' own learning services,
- to increase substantially the number of union members accessing learning,
- to assist unions to develop more strategic approaches to learning and related workplace issues and
- to help unions integrate their learning, bargaining and organising structures.

It will offer a range of services and consultative support in leadership development, skills strategy, training union activists and officials, and brokering learning provision, and will establish a learning and skills observatory, regional 'one-stop shops, and a union learning helpline and website.

The recent words of the current General Secretary of the TUC sum up the union perspective well.

I think it's no exaggeration to say that I see our work on learning as one of the most exciting developments in trade unionism really in a generation and it's a tremendously powerful example of the positive contribution the trade unions can make. In the last few years, we have seen countless union initiatives in this field. They have led to the establishment of over 120 workplace Learning Centres, hundreds of new learning agreements signed with employers in every part of the economy. Around 100,000 of our members a year are now benefiting from learning as a direct result of union-led initiatives and projects, and these have been driven by the network now of 8,000 union workplace learning representatives. Their job is to negotiate with their employers to boost training investment, to broker the provision of new opportunities with local colleges and other providers, and crucially to act as adviser and mentor to fellow workers, giving them the confidence to take the first steps back into learning. (Barber, 2005 and CIPD, 2005)

Following the election of the Labour government in 1997, unions have also been able to benefit from the operation of the publicly funded Union Learning Fund, which has been acknowledged as providing effective financial support to many union-led schemes to widen, diversify and extend learning opportunities for union members. A recent evaluation of the Union Learning Fund by researchers from the Working Lives Institute of London Metropolitan University confirms the findings of earlier research that the fund has had 'an enormous impact in terms of funding workplace learning projects, engaging adult learners and supporting the training of Union Learning Representatives'. However, there is still scope for improvement. (Wood and Moore, 2005) The researchers report that only a small proportion of unions have developed formal policies for workplace learning, the focus of union learning activity remains fairly narrowly concerned with certain types of course, (ICT, literacy and numeracy and some vocational programmes). According to Wood and Moore, only 4 per cent of learning representatives had been elected and new activists are less likely to feel well-supported by the union and to engage in other union activities. Most critically and more controversially, the authors conclude that 'union learning is not yet a mainstream union issue ... (and) the potential relationship between learning and organising has not yet been fully exploited' and that ' so far, union learning has been developed in isolation from wider union agendas and particularly from the bargaining agenda. (Wood and Moore, 2005: 41)

Some cynics might claim that this increased concern with learning has more or less coincided with the loss of trade union influence at work in the UK since the Conservative government legislative restrictions and changes of the 1980s and the halving of union membership and membership density over the past twenty years. Similarly, some critics of unions' engagement in learning and training have discerned in UK developments since the 1960s what they see as a blunting of the critical and radical edge of union education. However, for their part, British unions have understood that, increasingly, their members have looked to them for new sorts of union services and expect them to secure improvements in workplace learning opportunities, as part of their terms and conditions of work. They have also realised that active engagement with the learning agenda can contribute to a strengthening of union organisation and serve as an incentive to both recruitment and retention of union members.

Looking at some evidence

According to the evidence from the most recent National Adult Learning Survey (NALS), overall three-quarters of all adults reported undertaking some learning, of whatever kind, in the previous three years and 24 per cent said that they had undertaken no such learning. (DfES, 2003b) These latter are the adults classified as 'non-learners' in the rest of the NALS results, and the earlier caveats about this terminology need to be remembered. Half of all respondents had undertaken what the researchers defined as 'vocational learning only' in the last three years, and a further 18 per cent had undertaken both vocational and non-vocational learning in the same period. Looking to the future, two-thirds of those expecting to be still in paid work thought it fairly likely or very likely that they would be undertaking job-related learning, and just under one-third thought it unlikely. But here the differences between so-called 'learners' and 'non-learners' were stark: whilst three quarters of all 'learners' who intended to be working in the future expected to engage in job-related learning, less than one-third of the 'non-learners' had the same expectation, and two-thirds of them thought it not at all likely or not likely (DfES, 2003b: 16). Those who were most likely to expect to be undertaking job-related learning in the future had either already either followed vocational learning only in the past three years, or had undertaken both vocational and non-vocational learning (79 per cent in both cases), as against 38 per cent of those who had undertaken non-vocational learning only in the recent past.

Similar differences were found where future expectations of involvement in non-job-related learning were concerned: whilst 49 per cent of 'learners' expected to engage in such learning in the future, only 26 per cent of 'non-learners' shared this expectation and as many as 47 per cent of them said it was 'not at all likely' that they would undertake such learning in the future.

The NALS researchers also reported people's reasons for not engaging in learning and into the perceived obstacles to learning. Amongst the respondents classified as both 'learners' and 'non-learners', the main reason for not engaging in learning was a preference for spending their time doing other things and the lack of time because of family caring responsibilities. Both groups also reported the lack of time for learning because of work pressures, the difficulty in paying course fees and their lack of information about learning opportunities. 'Non-learners' were more likely than 'learners' to say they were 'not interested in learning' (29 per cent against 9 per cent), and more likely to say that were 'nervous about going back to the classroom' (24 per cent against 14 per cent). They were also slightly more likely to feel they 'didn't have the qualifications to get on the course' (21 per cent against 12 per cent) and more likely to feel they were 'too old to learn' (21 per cent against 7 per cent).

There were also some telling differences between the responses of men and women to the question of the perceived obstacles to learning. Whilst men were more likely than women to say that they preferred doing other things (36 per cent against 29 per cent) and were prevented from learning because of the time pressures of work (34 per cent against 25 per cent), women were more likely to cite lack of time to learn because of the family (26 per cent against 15 per cent) and children (20 per cent against 6 per cent). Women were also more likely than were men to say they were nervous about going back to the classroom (20 per cent against 12 per cent). The groups least likely to refer to nervousness about a return to study were those with qualifications at NVQ levels 5 and 4 (3 per cent and 5 per cent respectively) and the same groups were the least likely to refer to being too old to study. By contrast, those with only NVQ Level 1 qualifications, or with no formal qualifications at all, were the most likely to say that they preferred doing other things or were not interested in learning. The least qualified or unqualified were also more likely to say that had little time for learning because of the family, did not know about learning opportunities, were nervous about a return to the classroom, felt they lacked the qualifications to get on a course and were worried about being able to keep up with the course.

Further analysis of the NALS data showed a systematic link between respondents' age at leaving full-time education and previous qualification on the one hand and their recent involvement in learning on the other. Whilst 93 per cent of those who left at 21 or older reported involvement in learning of one kind or another in the last three years, the same was true for only 66 per cent of those who left at sixteen or younger. Those leaving full-time education at 21 or older were also much more likely to report involvement in vocational learning than those who left at 16 or younger (89 per cent as against 57 per cent). Similarly, whilst more than nine out of ten respondents with either NVQ levels 4 or 5 reported engagement in learning, only 29 per cent of those saying the had no qualifications had been so engaged. It is important to note here that, even some earlier qualification appears to be associated with reporting recent involvement in continuing learning: two-thirds of those already possessing an NVQ Level 1 had been involved in learning in the past three years and 85 per cent of those with a previous NVQ Level 2 had been so. Looking to the future, whilst more than four out of five of those respondents with an NVQ Level 4 or 5 expected to engage in vocational learning in the future, only one-third of those with no qualifications shared this expectation. Once again, though, some earlier qualification does seem to constitute an incentive to continue learning or to provide the confidence to do so: two-thirds of those with at least an NVQ Level 1 qualification expected to engage in vocational learning in the future.

The NALS data also draw attention to other differences and inequalities. First, people working in professional, managerial and other non-manual jobs were more likely to have been involved in recent learning, and especially vocational learning, than those in unskilled manual work. Second, those in full-time, part-time and self-employed paid work were rather more likely to have been in recent learning than unemployed respondents and far more likely to have been so than those who were already retired or who had responsibility for looking after the family. As many as 88 per cent of professionals and managers reported involvement in any recent learning and 83 per cent in vocational learning, as compared with 47 per cent of unskilled manual workers who had been involved in any learning and 36 per cent in vocational learning. The respondents most likely to have been involved in both any recent learning and vocational learning were employed either in professional occupations or in associate professional or technical work. As the authors of the NALS somewhat laconically observe, 'perhaps learning among (professionals and managers) is likely to be offered as part of the service contract by employers (as a form of payment or a compulsory part of the contract) or perhaps pursued by those in this group to maintain their usefulness to this contract'. (DfES, 2003b: 29) Just as likely, of course, is that involvement in the kinds of continuing learning reported in this survey is part of a wider picture of advantage and disadvantage and provides an insight into the characteristically relative positions of different groups in workplace hierarchies of power, status, resources and opportunity in the UK.

A somewhat different picture emerges from the other key source of evidence about engagement in adult learning in the UK, the annual survey undertaken by the highly respected National Institute for Adult Continuing Education. In their most recent analysis of results, *Better News this time?*, NIACE authors Fiona Aldridge and Alan Tuckett report that, altogether, 42 per cent of respondents said that they were either currently involved in learning or had undertaken learning recently (that is, in the past three years).(Aldridge and Tuckett, 2005: 4) This figure, the same as for the 2002 survey, represents a small (two percentage points) improvement on those reported in 1996 and 1999 but a four percentage point increase as compared with 2004. At the same time, the proportion reporting having undertaken no learning since leaving full-time education has remained more or less constant at 35 per cent. Since 1996, women's participation in current or recent learning has increased by five percentage points, whilst the corresponding figures for men have shown a reduction by three percentage points. In the latest report, 40 per cent of men and 43 per cent of women are reported as being currently or recently engaged in learning, a difference that is not statistically significant.

Perhaps the most telling data from the most recent NIACE study are those related to the rates of participation of different socio-economic groups. Whereas 56 per cent of those respondents from professional and senior managerial occupations (social classes A and B) reported involvement in current or recent learning, only 26 per cent of those respondents in unskilled occupations or from the lowest levels of subsistence, such as the long-term unemployed, people on benefits and pensioners (social class D and E) did so. Over the period from 1996, the reported participation in learning of skilled manual workers (social class C2) has increased by seven percentage points from 33 per cent to 40 per cent, and amongst part-time workers the increase over the same period has been from 42 per cent to 53 per cent, so that part-time workers are now as likely to report involvement in learning as their full-time colleagues (52 per cent and 53 per cent respectively). But the biggest differences in participation reported in the NIACE survey are those between those in work and the unemployed, those who are out of the workforce and retired people on the one hand and between younger adults (those under 25years of age) and older people (those older than 55) on the other.

Learning at work

There are also difficulties in getting an accurate and agreed picture of learning at work in the UK from the different surveys that are undertaken. For example, according to the National Employers Skills Survey 2003, (undertaken principally to ascertain the extent of employers' vacancies, skills shortages and gaps), about three in five establishments in England had provided training for their staff over the previous twelve months, although this rose to 97 per cent of those employing 500 or more staff. Results from this study indicated that, overall, 53 per cent of all employees had received some training in the past year and employers reported providing 'an average of five days' training to all employees. This equates to well over 100 million days of training per year.' (LSC, 2003: 21).

At the same time, according to a recent Learning and Training at Work survey of a sample of employers in England (Clarke, 2002, Department for Education and Skills), nine out of every ten employers offered their workers some kind of job-related training in 2002: amongst larger employers (those employing more than 100 staff), virtually all did so. About 50 per cent of employers reported providing off-the-job training and over three-quarters said that they provided training on the job. There were, according to this survey, substantial differences in the proportions offering both on- and off-the-job training between employers of different sizes and different industries. Whilst 88 per cent of companies employing more than 200 staff provided both kinds of training, only 48 per cent of those employing 5–24 staff did so. In transport, public administration and other services 72 per cent provided both kinds of training to their staff, whereas in distribution and consumer services, 45 per cent did so.

The Learning and Training at Work survey also reported that people working in smaller organisations who received any training from their employer appear to have enjoyed rather more days engaged in off-the-job training than did those working for big companies. Organisations employing 5–24 provided just over seven days off-the-job training per employee trained, as against just under five days per employee trained in companies employing 500 or more staff. At the same time, these differences largely disappeared where the average number of days of off-the-job training per employee was concerned. The average number of days per employee in all but the largest organisations was two, and for those in organisations employing 500 people or more, the average was 1.7 days.

Data collected about individuals learning opportunities at work through the regular Labour Force Survey also show marked differences between different occupations and grades of staff. Employees who already possess higher qualifications are more likely to receive training through work than their less-well-qualified colleagues are: 24 per cent of those with degree qualifications or above did so as against 5 per cent of those with none. Similarly, 'people in highly skilled jobs are more likely to receive training – those in professional occupational nearly four times as likely to receive training as those who work as operatives'. (Labour Market Trends, June 2002, 321)

Finally, perhaps the most striking statistic about learning opportunities at work is that, according to authoritative research, as many as 30 per cent of UK staff have never been offered any kind of training by their current employer – and that includes induction training, basic health and safety courses and any mandatory skills that might be required in certain occupations.

Workplace learning as participation

In a suggestive and challenging interpretation of data in the 2004 Learning at Work Survey, Felstead and colleagues draw on an earlier distinction made by Sfard between 'learning as acquisition' and 'learning as participation'. The researchers note the preferences of workers for a model of participative learning in which emphasis centres on workers 'taking part in activities, the fluidity of actions, the dialectical nature of the process of learning and the importance of the workplace as well as the classroom as a site for learning'. (Felstead *et al*, 2005: 12) The lower down the occupational hierarchy that workers found themselves, the more they were likely to be involved in, and to prefer, 'learning as participation'. By contrast, managers and professionals were more likely than workers in so-called 'operative' or 'elementary' occupations to favour training courses and skills acquired by studying or through 'learning by acquisition ', in which learning entails 'getting, attaining, accumulating, grasping and receiving' and which is more likely to be 'delivered, conveyed or facilitated by another'. Even so, occupational analysis of responses revealed that workers at all occupational levels recognised the value of learning through on-the-job experience.

The researchers conclude that 'policy discussions and debates about lifelong learning and the creation of a learning society are, therefore, poorly served by measures of learning which remain rooted in a tradition that only sees learning as the 'acquisition' of certificates, years spent in formal education and attendance at training events (on and off-the-job)'. Against this approach, their work highlights 'the contribution that the everyday experience of work can have in enhancing work performance through activities such as doing the job, being shown things, engaging in self-reflection and keeping one's eyes and ears open'. (Felstead *et al*, 2005: Conclusion, 26) These intriguing, if not altogether surprising, findings raise vital questions for workplace learning. First, how can different forms and process of learning, and the knowledge and practices arising from them be validated and bench-marked? Second, given that the weaknesses of learning methods dependent upon the 'acquisition' model have already been well rehearsed, is *anything* learned through the 'participative learning' process inherently valid, even if it can be shown by using other forms of evaluation than participants' attitudes to be mistaken, open to serious challenge, dangerous or even just plain wrong? Third, how can the participative model be further developed to secure what might be called 'third party' recognition of the knowledge, competences, knowhow and skills developed through this obviously preferred approach? Fourth, what exactly are the implications for elaborating a workplace learning pedagogy based on these findings and how can we be sure that those fellow workers who are the source of such participative learning are behaving consistently, honourably and are sharing accurate knowledge and skills?

Limited evidence and systematic inequalities

What all of this (admittedly limited) evidence suggests is, first, the need for much more systematic and extensive evidence about the range, scope, purposes, effects and patterns of worker engagement in workplace learning, of all kinds and modes. However, from the evidence already available, it is clear that the present situation reveals not just the existence of different *patterns* of learning amongst 'learners' and 'non-learners', and between the qualified, unqualified and lower qualified adults and amongst workers. It also draws attention to what appear to be *systematic inequalities in involvement in reported learning* amongst the population of working age. The data also confirm the observation, frequently made, that past patterns of and involvement in learning and achievement are a good guide to likely learning in the future. As Helena Kennedy once tellingly noted, 'If at first you don't succeed, you don't succeed' (Learning Works). Patterns of inequality in participation, enjoyment and achievement in learning that often start in relatively early childhood and at school. They are perpetuated, replicated and reinforced throughout life and, especially, at work and in the wider labour market. Moreover, as the research reported over a decade ago by Duncan Gallie and colleagues indicated, in a period of rapid and widespread change in industry, occupation and skills, workers with the lowest levels of recognised skill, the least training and the fewest opportunities to learn new skills are most likely to be left behind and further disadvantaged. (Penn *et al*, Chapter 2). It seems too that much rhetorical and enthusiastic employer and government commitment to workplace learning for all workers in the challenging circumstances of the coming 'Knowledge Economy' still needs to be matched by practical implementation and real achievements.

References

Aldridge, F and Tuckett, A (2005) *Better News this Time? The NIACE Survey on Adult participation in Learning* 2005, Leicester: NIACE.

Barber, B (2005), Speech to the national 'Advancing Enterprise' conference, 4 February, 2005.

CBI (2005) 'Teenagers leaving school without basic skills'. CBI Press Release, London, CBI August 2005.

CIPD (Chartered Institute of Personnel and Development), TUC and Learning and Skills Council (2005), *Trade Union Learning Representatives: the change agenda*, London: CIPD.

Clarke, A (2002) 'Who trains? Employers commitment to workforce development', *Labour Market Trends*, June 2002,319–22.

Confederation of British Industry (2001) *The CBI response to the consultation paper 'Providing Statutory Rights for Union Learning Representatives*, London: CBI.

Cross, J (2003) *Informal Learning: the other 80%*, www.internettime.com/learning/the other 80%.

Department for Education and Skills (2003a) *21st Century Skills. Realising our Potential. Individuals, Employers, Nation*, The Stationery Office, Cm 5810.

DfES (2003b), *National Adult Learning Survey, 2002*, London: DfES.

Ehrenreich, B (2002), *Nickel and Dimed: undercover in low-wage USA*, London: Granta.

Felstead, A, Fuller; A, Unwin, L, Ashton, D, Butler P and Lee, T (2005) *Better Learning, Better Performance: evidence from the 2004 Learning at Work Survey*, Leicester: NIACE.

Field, J (2000) *Lifelong Learning and the New Educational Order*, Stoke-on-Trent: Trentham Books.

Jarvis, P (2001), *Universities and Corporate Universities*, London: Kogan Page.

Kennedy, H (1997), *Learning Works*, Coventry: FEFC.

LSC (Learning and Skills Council) (2003) *National Employers Skills Survey 2003: Key Findings*, Coventry: LSC.

Penn, R, Rose, M and Rubery, J (eds) (1994) *Skills and Occupational Change*, Oxford: Oxford University Press.

Pilsbury, David (2002) *Learning and Training at Work 2001*, London: HMSO.

Senge, P (1990) *The Fifth Discipline: the Art and Practice of the Learning Organization*, London: Random House.

Senge, P, Kleiner, A, Roberts C, Ross, R, Roth, G and Smith, B (1999) *The Dance of Change: The Challenges of Sustaining Momentum in Learning Organizations*, London: Nicholas Brealey.

Stewart, T A (1997) *Intellectual Capital: the new Wealth of Organizations*, London: Nicholas Brealey.

TUC (2004) 'A Union Academy: adding value to the union card', Report and Proposal to the Executive Committee, 15 December 2004.

Wood, H and Moore, S (2005) *An Evaluation of the UK Union Learning Fund – Its Impact on Unions and Employers*, London: Working Lives Institute.

7
Should schools engage in widening participation?
Stephen Sheedy

The English have never been able to put in place an education system that guarantees that routes through formal learning from age 5 to 16 and beyond are reasonably consistent across geographical and socially defined areas. The differences between arrangements in different parts of the country become most marked at the critical period of transition from compulsory to post-compulsory schooling, and these structural arrangements, coupled with other factors relating to where a young person has been born, brought up and schooled, are likely to have some bearing on her or his attitude to staying on in higher education. A child born and educated in parts of north-east Leeds, which has very low participation rates in higher education, will have very reduced chances of encountering sixth form provision in the run up to completion of GCSE, for example. A child born in Liverpool will stand a good chance of attending one of a great number of schools with small school sixth forms, most of which perform consistently poorly at A-level year on year. A child born in North Hampshire will, by contrast, have a choice from up to seven high-performing colleges (sixth form, general FE and agricultural), when it comes to making a decision about where to continue with study.

There are further structural impediments to continuing with education once young people have made the decision to stay with formal learning beyond the age of sixteen. We learned in the summer of 2005 that Harry Potter has decided not to return to Hogwarts for his final year of sixth form and will, therefore, not complete his NEWTs. Ignoring the message this might send out to young people who may regard themselves as having, if not the destruction of Lord Voldemort to accomplish, far more important things to do than continue with study beyond 17, young Potter's decision reminded me of an article in *The Guardian* from August, 2003. Wendy Berliner wrote of another young man who, like Harry, had completed his first year of sixth form. Adam Philpott would take his AS levels and so achieve some certification unavailable to wizards, but would not be returning for his final year to his school in

Northamptonshire. Berliner addressed a number of factors contributory to Adam's decision, but her article directs us to the arrangements for Adam's learning:

> *By halfway though the year, he knew he wasn't going to take it any further. His school didn't have a sixth form, but was in a consortium with two others. His subjects were spread among three schools, separated by imperfect bus routes. He felt some of the staff at the two schools where he was a stranger treated him like a kid.*

The very structures of provision speak to young people about what they can expect, and what is expected of them, at sixteen and seventeen, and so about whether or not continuing into higher education is a realistic prospect for them at all.

Add to these structural messages the things that influential people tell them about their prospects and, my contention is, we have made it exceptionally difficult for young people in some parts of the country even to see higher education as a possibility. Moreover, should some of them manage to think of higher education, we tell them that it is not for them any way, since we already have too many people being educated beyond what is right for them. Education beyond the compulsory phases is clearly presented as belonging to some but not to all – and I am not here talking only about bright young people who miss out on the opportunity to go to the country's most selective universities.

We must not underestimate the power of some of the messages that young people in parts of the country, in the context of impedimentary structures of provision, may be picking up about what is appropriate for them in the post-compulsory phases. Indeed, the power of these messages makes it all the more important that schools and colleges mobilise partnerships to counter the negative attitudes to their prospects prevalent in the adult world. Starting with higher education itself, I will comment on messages from different sectors of education and beyond, and then on the role which we should play in widening participation.

In September 2004, Frank Furedi, Professor of Sociology at the University of Kent, produced what he called a confrontation with philistinism in the 21st century, but which might be thought of as a sustained tirade against dumbing-down in our universities and of our culture, and against the drive to widen access. *Where Have All the Intellectuals Gone?* was certainly not the first piece of work to challenge the assumptions behind moves to widen participation in higher education, nor was that its sole purpose, but it produced at least two very telling responses. Terry Eagleton welcomed it in the pages of *The New Statesman* as a vitally important attack on relativism. David Aaronovitch in *The Observer* saw

Furedi's position as champion of Truth (Furedi's capitalisation) and of a culture resistant to access by the idle, as actually predicated on his lack of enthusiasm for having a greater number of university students.

Here is a flavour of Furedi's attack on attempts to widen participation in higher education:

> ...*dumbing down is not an accidental by-product of the campaign to widen access to higher education, but the inevitable consequence of a perspective that views the objective of education as something that is external to education. In this case, access and inclusion is the goal and education is the means to achieve it.* (95)

I find it difficult to see how anything can contain within itself its own objective, which seems to be what Furedi desires for education. It is clear from his argument that what he despises in the academy of today is the triumph of utilitarianism, or rather the notion that higher education is used as an instrument to serve schemes for social engineering and the needs of the economy. As he warms to his attack, in the section entitled *The Culture of Flattery*, he takes no prisoners:

> *The access movement is profoundly hostile to pedagogic practices, standards and expectations that distinguish the university from other types of educational institutions. Research presented to the European Access Network in July 2001 criticized the 'enormous differences between the approaches and cultures of community education, further education and higher education'. The project of relaunching the university as a community college of further education represents the height of ambition of the access movement.* (117)

It would be pointless here to engage in argument with Furedi, and that is not why I have cited this text: rather, for me, the problem is that this message supports the reactions of people who choose to regard HE as too full already, either because they fear that universities do not have the capacity for continued growth or because they believe that there is a whole section of the community who cannot benefit from continuing in education beyond the compulsory stages. In doing so, they miss the opportunity to encourage others who need (and I use that word deliberately) higher education.

One contributory factor to the adoption of a stance antagonistic to widening participation (and, at the same time, a serious obstacle to understanding why participation should be widened and not simply increased) is the target that, by 2010, 50 per cent of 18–30 year-olds should have some experience of higher education. Government's failure to focus unashamedly on inequalities resulting from gender, race, physical ability or, perhaps most significantly, class has led to influential individuals and groups claiming that we have already gone far enough in increasing participation and that a whole swathe of other needs of the country are thereby being neglected. These claims are made without any apparent sense that a 50 per cent target, national though it is, has a wholly different meaning in Consett than in Winchester. Let me be clear about this: the variations in participation rates in higher education between different areas, even at the scale of electoral wards within one local authority, are such as to make it incontestable that social class plays an enormous part in the life-chances of individuals (HEFCE, 2005). The received wisdom is that this goes without saying, but when the effects of belonging to a particular class are combined with regional arrangements which increase inequality, and when central government makes little significant attempt to challenge such arrangements at the local level (often on the grounds that local people know best how to meet local needs) but sets national targets which mask scandalously variable performance, the needs of young people in some areas can disappear from sight.

Shortly before leaving the Learning and Skills Council, the former Chief Executive, John Harwood, went public with his belief that 50 per cent was far too high a target, and that what the country needed was not more graduates – we clearly had enough of them already – but more people qualified to Level 3 in areas of skills shortage, such as plumbing. It is not clear to me why plumbing always emerges as the quintessential skill shortage, but it does, and it is often opposed to philosophy. The English seem always unable to imagine that a philosopher can plumb or that a plumber can think systematically. Harwood's message is potentially damaging because it could encourage collusion in a culture of low aspiration in and for many of the nation's young people, and might reinforce the notion, prevalent where I was brought up, that the 'lower classes' should not look to higher education but to 'getting themselves a good trade'. Harwood was joined by at least one Chief Education Officer in contesting the value of the 50 per cent target and thereby the value of encouraging young people from areas of scandalously low participation to stay in education.

So far, then, we have heard powerful messages from figures in HE and FE expressing open antagonism to increasing participation and in so doing condemning widening participation. Incidentally, I think the distinction between these two concepts is valuable, because of the way an attitude to one can so clearly influence attitudes to the other, as seems to be the case with both Furedi and Harwood.

These are not, thankfully, the only messages from those involved in continuing education, but they probably support the voices which the young people on whom I am focusing hear most clearly.

Primary school heads in areas where there have been years of low participation in education beyond 16 and 18 may well tell you that in their efforts to raise aspirations among their pupils and their families they encounter a curious dynamic: the more the schools expect from the children, the greater the volume of complaint they receive from parents. Many parents do not see raising the aspirations of their children as in anybody's best interests.

Parents, uncles and aunts, whole communities are capable of giving a consistent message to young people, a message that gathers support from employers, careers advisers, education-business link organisations, the media, central government itself, the CBI, school governors and on and on, to the effect that many of them – the young people that is – should leave school at 16 to go into employment and perhaps develop their skills. Indeed, the regional development agencies are now saying that the drive for 'education, education, education' is effectively – and rightly – being replaced by a drive for 'skills, skills, skills'. If there are legacy issues in Tony Blair's final administration (that is to say, achievements that will diminish the likelihood of his being remembered solely for the Iraq War), then reform of the education system is a strong contender. However, in the push to implement the Level 2 and 3 skills agenda, reform ought not to cause a reaction against, or even precipitate neglect of, the need to widen participation in higher education. The government's 14–19 white paper could be read as deriving from resignation in the face of an overwhelmingly middle-class undergraduate and graduate population and the need for better-defined alternative pathways for those born to work with their hands. In other words, central government itself may have lost faith in the 50 per cent per cent target, without replacing it with aims to redress the scandalous imbalance in access.

There are other sources of messages for young people and, while Middlesex University's advertising on MTV is impressive, some key agencies seem not to have young people and higher education embedded in the stories they tell about themselves. It can be quite a salutary exercise to imagine yourself as a sixteen year-old who knows nothing at all about higher education for some or all of the reasons I have sketched above and then use the Internet to find out about higher education and what it might offer you. Type in 'higher education' or 'university' and you will find absolutely nothing that doesn't assume you already know what you are looking for. Try the 'Connexions' website and you will be hard-pressed to find a single reference to higher education without some serious digging. Enter 'Modern Apprenticeships' and you will get a very clear picture of what's on offer and how to go about accessing it with no reference whatsoever to higher education opportunities beyond the apprenticeship itself. I tried typing in 'degrees' and the first result I got was from *www.phonydiplomas.com*:

> ### Welcome to Phony Diplomas!
> *Your online source for authentic fake high school diplomas, phony transcripts, quality fake diploma and fake college diplomas.*

Would young people already know about 'Action on Access' or 'Aimhigher'? The latter's website is pleasingly user-friendly for young people, but I could not get to it using any of the routes which seemed to me to be obvious. It would seem that if you don't know your way around the system already, or you are not being guided by someone who does and who believes in your ability to gain from higher education, you've no business trying to find the route in – not even electronically.

What exactly, then, faces the young man or woman who, having received our messages loud and clear, attends a state secondary school without its own sixth form in an area where there is little sixth-form provision, or where it is patchy, or where the only post-16 provision is at a general FE college, probably doing its best for 16–18 year-olds but with such a divergent mission that it cannot concentrate on widening participation into higher education? The absence of coherently designed provision country-wide means that while one group of young people (the more so if high-achieving and mobile by the age of 16) will have a choice of several state-system sixth-form or other colleges on completing key stage 4, others will have no consciousness at all that continuing education is for them, and will never have been introduced to the notion of going to a university or even of 'having an experience of higher education' by the age of 30. What's more, they may well have been actively discouraged from staying in school beyond 16. Higher education is nowhere on the horizon.

In this context, it is clear that *schools* must engage in widening participation, since they are almost certainly the most powerful agencies able to combat the weight of opposition to some young people's thinking of themselves as capable of gaining from education beyond 16 or 18. Many schools and colleges are doing a lot of work to encourage young people to stay with education, and not just because of funding for institutions. What is now clear is that the messages against continuing education are best countered by schools working in partnership.

There is, of course, something else needed: leadership. If many young people cannot navigate the routes and overcome the impediments I have touched on above without the help of adults who have influence over them, faith in their ability to benefit, belief in their right to access and a conviction that it really matters that young people should not be deprived of the opportunity of higher education, schools have to be brave enough to put participation in education beyond 16 and 18 very high on their agenda. Many of the schools in the areas I have mentioned lack the confidence to make higher education a priority, committed as they are to keeping their head above water with GCSE performance and the accompanying league tables. Many of them have been left to work on their own in very difficult circumstances without the capacity to build the kind of partnerships that might allow them to look to a future for their pupils beyond school leaving. It is to be hoped that 'Aimhigher' can help such institutions develop capacity for working in partnership and that school leaders can make higher education part of the stories that schools tell about themselves. Political leadership is also critically important, but schools cannot hang about waiting for reorganisation of provision to remove impediments to students' progress.

Schools and colleges must have very clearly stated purposes and narratives about themselves which everyone can understand and which include the aim of helping people to stay with education for as long as they can benefit from doing so. Moreover, those narratives must be shared by partners who have an influence on the decisions young people and their parents make about their engagement with education.

Clarity of purpose and the stories that schools and their partners tell about themselves and their successes are essential in building confidence among staff and pupils. This is true also for what higher education institutions define as their purpose and what stories they tell about themselves.

When Steven Schwartz was concluding his work on making admission to university more fair, he spoke to a number of groups around the country about, among other things, our failure to recognise how the United Kingdom had changed in the post-war years and to see the importance of higher education in bringing people to an understanding of each other's culture, background and meaning in the world we inhabit. Furedi would almost certainly see such a 'purpose' as instrumentalist and philistine, but if higher education does lead to greater tolerance and understanding among its students, it is only in the past 40 or fewer years that we have come to understand that and it may now be time for higher education itself to trumpet that effect of widening participation: higher education cannot exist solely for the purposes of supplying the nation with public intellectuals.

Indeed, it is surely partly because higher education is, if not identified with, at least confused with, universities as research institutions, that higher education institutions can join schools and colleges in sending out the wrong messages to young people. What has happened to an education system in which, for example, a perceived national skills shortage must be addressed by schools and FE colleges, while higher education, in so far as it is all provided by universities, is thought of as needing to concentrate on research and having little or no role in developing skills directly related to vocations or occupations and, in any event, is often perceived as undervaluing teaching and learning? If there is to be a call to schools and FE colleges to lead confidently to counter the powerful messages against widening participation, then there must be a similar call to leaders in higher education to make widening participation central in the stories they tell about their functions, purposes and aims.

It is not my intention to pillory Furedi, but I would like to return to one reaction to the publication of *Where Have All the Intellectuals Gone?* before concluding. David Aaronovitch, in his review, purported to have glimpsed Furedi's underlying attitude:

> *Thus Furedi argues, on broadening access, that, 'in principle, creating equal opportunities for all is a worthwhile objective. Increasing public participation in cultural and intellectual life is a goal that anyone with democratic leanings can support.*
> *The pusillanimous words 'worthwhile' and 'can support' stick out, standing in place of a truly progressive 'essential' and 'must fight for'. Furedi will deign to tolerate democratisation, but only if the would-be participants match his exacting standards.*

The warmth of Furedi's attack clearly invites a warm response and I'm afraid I can't resist quoting Aaronovitch's conclusion, even at the risk of a loss of measure:

> *The 'cultural elites' who want broadened access to higher education want it because they think the experience benefits both the student (who – as a citizen – has something of a right to be so benefited) and the society. The people who don't want it, it strikes me, are still those who would like to maintain their privileges, safe from scrutiny or (a word that Furedi hates) accountability. They don't want the unwashed walking through their corridors or inspecting their books.*
> *Too late, Frank. We aren't going back to Cambridge 1936, to that fabulous race of warrior dons who knew everything, to the days when intellectuals were intellectuals and women were their wives and mistresses, to a world when some people always got to talk and never had to listen.*

It is not simply that the messages young people receive are confusing: there is, indeed, much confusion, but two very clear messages emerge. One group of young people is told that higher education is the natural route for them to take, part of their birthright: another group is told very clearly that it is not for them. In the face of that scandal, of course schools, with as many powerful partners as they can muster, should engage in widening participation.

References

Aaronovitch, D (2004) 'The thinking classes: too clever by half', *The Observer*, 12 September 2004.
Berliner, W (2003) 'Children still do not want to go to university', *The Guardian*, 4 August 2003
Furedi, F (2004) *Where Have all the Intellectuals Gone?* London: Continuum.

8
The National Compact Scheme

Ceri Nursaw

Many studies have shown that higher education participation in England is not equal across different groups within society. Within the UK, the discussion of participation has, in the last few years, largely focused on the relative participation by different socio-economic groups. It has been often reported in the UK that the socio-economic groups IIIM, IV and V have lower participation rates than social groups I and II. This was crystallised in the Higher Education White Paper (DfES, 2003) which stated that the 'social class gap among those entering higher education is unacceptably wide. Those from the top three social classes are almost three times as likely to enter higher education as those from the bottom three'. The government proposed several ways in order to address this inequity including ensuring that admissions were fair, raising the aspirations and achievement of young people, and requiring Access Agreements which would be the gateway through which higher education could raise its fees.

These Access Agreements (OFFA, 2004) were required in March 2005 and institutions were asked to set out how they would ensure that they gained or retained a diverse and socially inclusive undergraduate student cohort in light of changes to the student funding arrangements in 2006. In order to gain agreement to charge 'top-up' fees, institutions were required to have a clear outreach programme and provide bursaries to those from low-income families. This, however, was just the latest in a long line of initiatives designed to encourage (require) institutions to ensure they were socially inclusive. Prior to the HE Act, HEFCE provided institutions with 'postcode premium' funding (HEFCE, 1999) designed to support institutions to further widen participation and support those students from a widening participation background already at the institution. HEFCE also published performance indicators (HEFCE, 2003a) which showed the level of participation by socio-economic groups across all institutions. All this has ensured that institutions responded to the widening participation agenda.

Higher education has responded to the inequity in social class in a myriad of ways. All higher education institutions now have outreach programmes into (typically) local schools and colleges in which they run activities with the students to raise their aspirations and achievement. Whilst this has had some impact on a national level it is difficult for individual HEIs to measure the difference it is making to their own institution and student profile. Therefore, increasingly, institutions are looking to ensure that they identify, and admit, students who have the potential (and ability) to succeed in higher education. In order to do this many institutions have adopted within their 'widening participation strategies' targeted compacts and 'special consideration' arrangements. These compacts and 'special consideration' arrangements are aimed at providing a route into higher education for those that have not fully demonstrated potential or ability through traditional means which typically means A-level (predicted) grades.

Yet whilst most institutions have adopted some form of compact or special consideration there is much confusion surrounding them, their scope and their purpose. There is no consistent definition or framework of what a compact scheme entails and because of this there is often confusion not only amongst the learners but also within the institutions themselves. This paper covers the work of the *National Compact Scheme*, which is one year into a two-year funded research project. It raises some issues that will need to be addressed both within the research and by the sector itself over the coming months.

Background

Compacts and special consideration arrangements are not new to the sector. It could be argued that many adult access programmes were an initial form of compact. However, their use for 'young' entrants has increased in line with increasing political focus on this age group and as such has raised questions regarding their appropriateness and use.

In 2003, Professor Steven Schwartz was asked by the then Secretary of State for Education and Skills, Charles Clarke, to lead an independent review on admissions to higher education. The resulting report *Fair admissions to higher education: recommendations for good practice* (DfES, 2004) determined five principles which should form the basis for fair admissions. Schwartz also made some wider recommendations, which included special admissions arrangements (this includes compacts). It was suggested that it was 'timely to review special consideration arrangements to ensure that there is equality of opportunity across the country for people in similar circumstances to participate in schemes giving preferential treatment or to be considered under special measures'. This review is the National Compact Scheme, which is sector-led (by the University of Leeds) and has been funded by Aimhigher (as a national project) since August 2004.

The aim of the review is to seek to develop and provide a framework for a collaborative compact scheme that can operate nationally across the HE sector. The intention is to have one framework, understandable by teachers, school students and the institutions themselves – thereby offering transparency and fairness. Its national basis is intended to ensure that young people have the mobility to move to institutions of their choice. To inform the framework the project has reviewed current practices to see if they meet the needs of young people and are in line with recommendations and principles set out in the Schwartz Report.

The work over the last twelve months has focused on the review of current practices. As we, as a sector, seek to define a common definition and process the research has already thrown up many issues which will impact directly on the admissions process and current widening participation strategies.

Current sectoral response

The current sectoral response to widening participation has been affected by the fact that higher education is dominated by students from the socio-economic groups I and II, that is those from professional and non-manual backgrounds. In 2001/02 only 26 per cent of young first-degree entrants to full-time degree courses came from the socio-economic groups IIIM, IV and V (HEFCE, 2003a). This dominance is more stark in 'selective' institutions, with some universities having between only 9 and 15 per cent of students from lower socio-economic backgrounds.

We have, therefore, seen the development of compacts occur for a variety of reasons:

- To encourage more young people from 'non-traditional' backgrounds into higher education[1]
- To break down existing perceptions of a particular institution and encourage young people to go to universities they may not have normally considered
- To support young people from non-traditional backgrounds into higher education by offering a more individualised supportive route.

Processes vary between different schemes and different institutions; the National Compact Scheme has identified four broad approaches:

- Individuals who meet specified criteria are considered for admissions adjustments.
- Individuals who attend particular schools and colleges and who successfully complete specified activities qualify for admissions adjustments.
- Individuals who meet specified criteria are considered and may receive conditional offers which include admissions adjustments. A condition of the offer is the successful completion of specified activities which trigger the admissions adjustments.
- Individuals who undertake additional periods of study (such as extra foundation year) are eligible for adjustments to the standard offer.

(University of Leeds, 2005)

The size, scope and arrangements for admissions entitlements and adjustments again vary considerably. At the start of the review we were aware of the large number of compact schemes operating across England. Many of these schemes are recognised nationally as innovative and highly influential in widening participation to higher education for non-traditional groups. However, the numbers involved are often very small. The compacts range from broad cross-institutional schemes to promote entry to a mix of courses to those that are designed and implemented for one particular programme of study. Some award 'credit' for certain activities, others expect participation at particular events. However, all focused on a 'local' area and promoted the scheme with particular schools and colleges. And, of course, all were concerned with targeting those from non-traditional backgrounds.

Whilst there were commonalities there have also been many differences which, when reviewing why compact schemes have been adopted and the approaches taken, have raised issues regarding the admissions process as well as the nature of widening participation and the strategies employed to develop a more inclusive higher education sector.

Questions raised

It should be noted that the questions and responses raised here are initial thoughts: the National Compact Scheme (NCS) is still continuing its analysis. The NCS has started from the value position that compacts should be central to the higher education sector's desire to widen participation and become more inclusive. Compacts cannot, and should not, be a bolt-on activity peripheral to the rest of the institution's work to widen participation. Yet the way in which they operate and the way they are embedded into the work of the institution are where difficulties often arise.

Understanding what is, or is not, a compact or special consideration scheme has proved one such difficulty, as there is not one standard established and shared definition. Schwartz 'recognises that compact and related schemes do much good work in encouraging and supporting learners in progressing to higher education and supports the continuation of this work'. The report describes a compact as a measure 'that confers an advantage in the admissions process' on those in disadvantaged circumstances or from under-represented groups. 'Conferring an advantage' is, however, a problematic phrase and implies an 'unfair' system which is not equitable to all – as some will achieve an advantage. But this is the crux of the issue – *do we want to address the inequities in participation by direct action at admission to higher education or do we subscribe to the belief that all have the same chances to demonstrate their abilities and full potential?*

Of course this is not only an English (UK) issue but, as Watson (2005) argued, the 'weight of evidence suggests that the key divide around the work is … socio-economic circumstances'. The USA has wrestled with the problem for many decades, initially around race (and continues to do so). Its higher education sector has many institutions offering as an entry requirement only the 'ability to benefit'. However, in reality the 'elite' institutions in which competition for places is fierce do have entry requirements. And it is in these 'elite' institutions that there exists a 'persistence and reproduction of a social-class-based stratified system of postsecondary opportunity that thwarts meritocratic ideals' (McDonough, 1997). In response, institutions have tried in the USA to engage in 'positive action' to ensure that their enrolments engender a more inclusive university. This is now being rejected as there is growing public support for notions of 'meritocratic ideals' and individual fairness. However, as the USA embraces this it still sees inequity in terms of participation by social class, particularly in selective/'elite' institutions.

Here, the government has been vocal in what they see as a fundamental need for universities to be inclusive to all socio-economic groups, even to the extent of publicly criticising individual institutions on their composition. Speaking about one admissions system Chancellor Gordon Brown said it was 'more reminiscent of the old-boy network and the old school tie than genuine justice in our society'. However, they have yet to engage in a debate on how all universities can be more inclusive or operate 'social justice' apart from encouraging institutions to provide bursary support and undertake aspiration-raising activities in schools. We need to recognise (and any definition for a compact needs to take into account) that we are dealing with 'change'. Compacts and special admissions are *not* about preserving the status quo but are about social change both within our universities and beyond. It is wrong and less than straightforward not to recognise this and we must not shy away from the fact that a compact means that some applicants who formerly obtained a place (particularly on competitive courses) may not do so in the future unless the system expands. We cannot continue to treat people the same, as all that will happen is a perpetuation of the current system. However, this is not about social engineering but it does mean (as Schwartz recommends) taking into account contextual factors and engaging in holistic assessment.

We need to separate the issue of compacts being part of an institution's widening participation strategy and admissions policy and ask: *should compacts be an intrinsic part of widening participation and admissions?* At first this appears to be a very desirable position as we seek to develop long-term relationships with young people which, over a period of time, will raise their aspirations to higher education. It is almost self-evident that taking a broader view of an applicant (that is contextual factors as part of the holistic assessment) needs to be an intrinsic part of the institution's targeted work with local schools and colleges. However, when applications to courses are considered, all applicants irrespective of the schools and colleges they attend need to be treated equally and given the same opportunities to demonstrate their abilities and full potential.

It is accepted that in order to be equitable and fair to all applicants they must be treated in a consistent manner at application and when making an offer. Student A is in a school targeted by the University of Poppleton, has no family history of higher education and is in a single-parent family whose sole means of support is Incapacity Benefit. Student A participates in Poppleton's compact scheme because she attends one of Poppleton's targeted schools. Student B goes to a school which has not been targeted by the university and thus does not know about the compact scheme, but his home circumstances match those of Student A. Both Student A and Student B wish to do the same course at the University of Poppleton.

Student A is part of a *proactive* relationship with the university that is looking to widen access. Student B is part of a *reactive* relationship which begins when he makes his UCAS application. In some schemes Student A will, at the point of application, have already participated in some type of credit-bearing course that forms the basis for the compact, but Student B will not have had that opportunity. Therefore, Student B will be disadvantaged at the point of application and has not been treated in the same way as Student A. It is, therefore, important that we continue to work to widen participation but ensure that at the point of admission all applications are treated equally and have the chance to be assessed holistically with contextual factors taken into account. This chance of a compact offer should be open to all applicants. We need to ensure that there is fairness to all with similar backgrounds. It is untenable that as we seek to widen participation we inadvertently create a biased system that does not treat all applicants with similar backgrounds the same. If one considers further the case of Student C who wants to go to a university other than Poppleton but finds she has to participate in a different type of compact, the argument in favour of a national scheme which is fair to all at application becomes very clear.

This has implications for both recruiting and selecting universities/courses. For recruiting universities/courses, compacts are often used as a means to draw into the institution motivated students who have demonstrated the skills to succeed at higher education and are from 'non-traditional' backgrounds. This avoids (or diminishes) the need for clearing. Increasingly they are looking to 'tie' the young person into their institution and as part of this often make early offers. Selecting universities/courses wish to broaden their intake to reflect the societies in which they operate and identify the 'brightest and best'. They, therefore, wish to identify the young people early so that they can be sure of their potential. This results in an emphasis by both on targeting, which can exclude similar young people from other schools and colleges. A common framework for compacts is, therefore, desirable so that individuals can have the mobility to move to other institutions and courses which best suit their needs. But we also need to consider the timing of the offer and at what point individuals are invited to join the compact. Making all offers during standard application timescales is likely to be the best way of ensuring that all applicants are treated equally and consistently. It would also ensure that institutions move away from a recruitment focus to a focus on what is best for the individual. Such a change should also open up higher education to more disadvantaged individuals.

In terms of opening the doors to higher education compacts have been quite successful, although it is easy to exaggerate the number and scale of the compacts currently in operation. For institutions which make two offers to applicants – the standard offer and the compact offer – it has been found (and more investigation is needed) that students often accept the standard offer only and come in through 'traditional' routes. Anecdotal evidence suggests that the students have been made to 'feel special' and have had their aspirations raised by individual attention and, often a more structured and supported route through the admissions process. This does then require us to ask what is the purpose of compacts – *is it to encourage people from disadvantaged backgrounds to apply to higher education or is it to ensure that we recognise the full potential of an applicant in the admissions process?* Surely it is both; and we must ensure that there are appropriate, and perhaps different, strategies at the two distinct stages of pre-application and application and admission.

The questions that have been raised by the review of compacts and special admission arrangements have been broader and deeper than we expected and have posed real and challenging questions about what is the true practice of widening participation within the sector. Compacts are integral to both an institution's widening participation strategy and admissions policy. It is important that these two frameworks are carefully and appropriately structured so that as a sector we operate fairly and consistently but, most importantly, in the best interests of the individual.

This paper has not touched on some of the other issues that have been raised, such as:

- Is this approach transferable to adult learners and part-time study?
- Do we need 'someone' to implement a national scheme?
- How do we address vocational routes?
- What is the role of information, advice and guidance?

The final report on the National Compact Scheme will be published in Spring 2006.

Note

1   Whilst many of the compacts focus on raising aspiration to higher education within their programmes it has yet to be seen how this affects absolute numbers to higher education and whether this is just 'preaching to the converted'.

References

DfES (Department for Education and Skills) (2003) *The future of higher education,* Cm 5735, London: The Stationery Office.

DfES (Department for Education and Skills) (2004) *Fair admissions to higher education: recommendations for good practice,* DfES / Admissions to Higher Education Steering Group.

HEFCE (Higher Education Funding Council for England) (1999) *Widening participation in higher education* May 99 / 33, Bristol: HEFCE.

HEFCE (Higher Education Funding Council for England) (2003a) *Performance indicators in higher education: 2000-01 and 2001-02*, 2003/59, Bristol: HEFCE.

HEFCE (Higher Education Funding Council for England) (2003b) *Funding for widening participation in higher education*, 2003/14, Bristol: HEFCE.

McDonough, P M (1997) *'Choosing colleges: how social class and schools structure opportunity'*, Albany, NY: SUNY Press.

Office for Fair Access (2004) *Producing access agreements: OFFA guidance to institutions*, Bristol: OFFA.

Watson, D (2005) 'Overview: telling the truth about widening participation', in G Layer (ed), *Closing the equity gap*, Leicester: NIACE.

9

The implications of widening participation for learning and teaching

Liz Thomas

Introduction

Widening participation in higher education is about student success[1] as well as access for students from under-represented groups. In the UK, however, there is a strong focus on aspiration-raising and access initiatives, rather than interventions designed to improve retention, success and progression. Recent research (Thomas *et al*, 2005a) received 141 examples of widening participation practice from higher education institutions (HEIs) and partnerships from across the country. The responses were categorised into four areas: pre-entry, access to higher education, retention and success, and enhancing employability. Of the interventions 64 per cent related to pre-entry activities and nearly one quarter (23 per cent) focused on access; very few examples centred on retention and success (6 per cent) or employability (7 per cent). This suggests there is a far greater emphasis on outreach as opposed to in-reach (Murphy *et al*, 2002). This focus reflects government policies in England, which have centred on raising aspirations, outreach work and fair access through Aimhigher, the Schwartz Report recommendations, Access Agreements and the Office for Fair Access (OFFA). There is very little national policy emphasis on developing a transformative model of widening participation which values and benefits from greater student diversity (see Jones and Thomas, 2005).

The focus of this paper is on the implications of widening participation for learning and teaching, as this is a key aspect of the student experience within HE. How learning is experienced can impact on academic achievement and social engagement, which reinforce each other and reduce the likelihood of both voluntary and involuntary withdrawal

(Tinto, 1993; Thomas, 2002). The classroom is a very important intervention site, especially for students from under-represented groups. This is not only because learning is the *raison d' être* of HE, but new student cohorts are likely to have less engagement in other aspects of HE life, and therefore the academic sphere gains greater significance. Many new students study at their local higher education institution, and thus they do not live in HE accommodation, but rather have to commute to participate. This excludes them from many social and communal aspects of the HE experience. This is reinforced by a high dependence on 'part-time' employment for financial survival. They may have to work longer hours than their peers, and perhaps more crucially, it is of greater importance to them, so they cannot jeopardise it – thus employment may have to take precedence over study and other engagement with HE experiences. Furthermore, some new students have additional responsibilities, including childcare, care of relatives, and other social pressures which restrict their full participation in all aspects of higher education. Students can make friends through their learning, as well as develop their knowledge and understanding, and this becomes a virtuous circle.

The first section of the paper reviews the research evidence about the need for institutional change in relation to learning and teaching, and identifies some of the reasons why there may be a lack of development in this sphere of widening participation. The second section reviews the research evidence regarding curriculum development, teaching strategies and assessment to support academic success to identify what changes the research suggests are required. The paper then briefly examines institutional practices in relation to widening participation by considering the recent study funded by Universities UK (UUK) and the Standing Conference of Principals (SCOP) to assess the sector's progress in developing successful approaches to widening participation (Thomas *et al*, 2005a). The paper concludes by identifying some key areas for development in relation to learning and teaching.

Learning, teaching and institutional change

A review of the literature indicates that institutional change is necessary to make widening participation a reality (Marks 2000, 2002; Bowl, 2001; Foskett 2002; Thomas, Woodrow and Yorke, 2002). Researchers conclude that learning and teaching environments are highly influential on students' success (e.g. Laing and Robinson, 2003). Davies (1999) writing the in the FE context, asks whether poor student retention is 'a problem of quality or of student finance'. Drawing on questionnaire research with 415 students, 34 per cent of whom had withdrawn, he argues that although financial hardship is pervasive it is not the primary cause of student drop-out. Rather, issues relating to pedagogy, practical organisational issues and the support provided have the most pronounced impact on retention rates. In the HE sector, Thomas (2002), drawing on focus groups with 32 students, reports that finance is important, but relations between students and with staff can be much more influential in students' decisions to remain in HE. Rhodes and Nevill (2004) reach similar conclusions using a student survey: debt and money worries are significant, but so are learning and teaching issues. They conclude that 'many of the facets identified fall within institutional control and can be managed in order that both 'traditional' and 'non-traditional' students may achieve integration, maintain their personal vision and be retained'.

Research about specific student groups in HE repeatedly finds that the learning environment must change for these students to feel integrated and to reach their academic potential. For example, Bamber and Tett (2001) conclude that it is essential to take into account the wider socio-economic context of students within the learning and teaching context in HE. Parker *et al* (2005) find that those institutions that have been successful so far in widening participation have developed a diversity of teaching and other practices that are appropriate to the needs of a mass sector.

Research about learning and teaching suggests that not only is this a highly important area of institutional change, but it will benefit all students. For example, Preece and Godfrey (2004) argue that expertise in academic literacy practices is crucial for all students to succeed and to achieve their full potential. They advocate a more explicit and dynamic approach to the teaching of academic literacy practices. In relation to disabled students Tinklin *et al* (2004) found that learning and teaching issues need to be embedded into all institutional policies and procedures and these will be of benefit to all students (see also Avramidis and Skidmore, 2004).

Many researchers, however, report a lack of learning and teaching development and institutional change. Layer *et al* (2002) found that less than one-third of HEIs have explicit links between learning and teaching and widening participation strategies. Longden (2000) concludes that the HE sector wants to retain its elitist traditions and so resists change. Foskett (2002) argues that the widening participation agenda has not impacted on institutional cultures because of the project-based nature of much of its activity. Bowl (2001) suggests that the 'deficit model', which problematises the student, rather than seeking institutional change, is dominant, and thus institutions do not perceive the need to change. Certainly, Clegg *et al* (2003) found that when teaching staff blamed Asian undergraduate students for having poor motivation 'it became clear that the discussion of motivation was overlaid by a racialising discourse, which allowed some staff to present the issue as an "Asian problem"'. Similarly, Davies (1999) found a mismatch between staff assessment of the reasons for early withdrawal and students', with the former implicitly blaming students and the latter identifying learning and teaching issues.

In addition to not wanting to change, or not realising the need to change, some staff and institutions may not know *how* to change, either because they do not know what new student cohorts want, or because they lack the skills and capacity. Foskett (2002) argues that there is limited awareness of the complexity of needs and wants of current non-participants (see also Thomas *et al*, 2005a). Dogra *et al* (2004) note that there is great uncertainty about 'what constitutes diversity teaching' (4), and this may be reinforced by limited participation in staff development activities to address this gap. Srivastava (2002) found that staff development to support widening participation is weak, and often based on voluntary participation.

How should curricula, pedagogies and assessment be reformed to support widening participation?

In this section research evidence about curriculum development, teaching strategies and assessment to support academic success is reviewed to identify what changes the research suggests are required. Based on this review six issues are identified and discussed here:

- induction and the first year experience;
- introducing diversity into the curriculum;
- 'employability' and progression;
- student-centred interactive learning;
- providing integrated academic and pastoral support;
- alternative assessment strategies.

1. Induction and the first year experience

Traditionally, HEIs have offered new students a Welcome or Freshers' week on arrival. There is now greater recognition of the need to induct students into the wider HE environment and provide information about the expectations and culture of HE (Layer *et al*, 2002: 91). Some institutions are now recognising the value of a 'longer and thinner' induction that starts earlier and lasts longer than a week (Layer *et al*, 2002; Thomas *et al*, 2002b). This provides a more effective opportunity for new students to assimilate and make sense of the information provided, to socialise with the staff and existing students through a range of activities and to feel that they belong in the HE community at their institution (Thomas *et al*, 2005b). Wallace (2003), for example, shows the importance of the first-year experience, and how this requires well-designed policy and practice.

2. Introducing diversity into the curriculum

The higher education curriculum is informed by white, western, middle class and male ways of knowing. It is argued that the curriculum ought to be culturally relevant to support widening participation and to prepare graduates for living and working in a diverse society. For example, Dibben (2005) explores the influence of socio-economic background on students' experiences of studying music. A small number of students felt that they did not fit into the department, and believed the curriculum was 'too traditional' (as it focused on classical music). In relation to working-class mature students Bamber and Tett (2001) recommend that relevant course material is used. Similarly, Haggis and Pouget (2002) suggest that to support first-generation entrants links need to be made between the curriculum and students' own experiences and views of the world. Houghton and Ali (2000) explore the development and delivery of a culturally relevant curriculum with Asian women, and encourage students to offer feedback about their educational provision to assist future development of the curriculum.

In the UK the General Medical Council (1993) has promoted the teaching of 'cultural diversity' in the medical undergraduate curriculum, and states that 'students should have acquired respect for patients and colleagues that encompasses, without prejudice, diversity of background and opportunity, language, culture and way of life'. Dogra *et al* (2004) find that between 1995 and 2003 there has been an increase in diversity teaching in medical schools in the UK and Eire but, 'further work needs to be undertaken to embed cultural diversity teaching within the medical undergraduate curriculum and to ensure it is valued, by staff and students' (7). Hope and Sebastian (2000) demonstrate that inclusivity workshops for first-year engineering students, which focus on culture, race and cross-cultural communication, assist students to work together more effectively within HE *and* prepare them for employment in engineering teams after graduation.

3. 'Employability and progression'

Blackwell *et al* (2001) argue that the HE curriculum should offer students the opportunity to reflect on employment and other experiences to explore the learning and skills development that is involved in these activities. Barrie (2005) similarly argues that the undergraduate curriculum from the first year onwards should assist students to develop 'graduate attributes', which, amongst other things, will assist them in future employment, and life more generally. The need for learning and teaching to develop personal, social and employability skills is supported by empirical research with 400 students at the start of their course and following graduation (Glover *et al*, 2002). Glover *et al* argue that the extension of partnerships between higher education and employers are essential to improve the employability of graduates. Purcell *et al* (2002) suggest that work placements offer both students and employers opportunities: students gain valuable skills and demonstrable competencies, and employers are able to recruit graduates from a wider pool. In addition, students are increasingly engaged in part-time employment, and so this offers a way to capitalise on this experience, and better prepare students for graduation (not just in terms of employment by more generally). While students from lower socio-economic groups are likely to be engaged in higher levels of paid employment, it should not be assumed that they have more to gain from such curriculum innovations than other students (Jones, 2006). Thus, the research indicates that part of the learning experience should prepare students for graduation in the broadest sense.

4. Student-centred interactive learning

There is a consensus that interactive as opposed to didactic teaching improves academic success and promotes the inclusion of learners who might feel like outsiders (Bamber and Tett, 2001; Haggis and Pouget, 2002; Thomas, 2002; Parker *et al*, 2005). According to Warren (2003)[2] 'case studies of students' learning behaviours and outcomes (Leftwich, 1987; Evans, 1990; Sheppard and Gilbert, 1991; Hellmundt *et al*, 1998; Ramsay *et al*, 1999) reveal that where teaching entails student-centred, discussion-based and group-based activities in seminars/small-group tutorials which offer safe and supportive learning environments:

- students' participation and interaction is enhanced;
- students experience a higher degree of comfort to express their ideas;
- communication among students in culturally diverse classes is improved;

- adjustment to university study is eased (for both international as well as local students);
- a shift towards deep learning can be facilitated, where space is created for learners to test out new concepts;
- there can be increased motivation, quality of discussion and level of analysis'.

(Warren, 2003: 3).

The benefits of student-centred learning that includes greater staff-student and peer interaction can be understood in relation to the social and emotional dimension of learning. This engagement influences students' sense of belonging and their motivation and achievement (Thomas, 2002; Askham, 2004; Košir and Pečjak, 2005). Pedagogies that involve students as active learners, rather than recipients of knowledge, show respect for students' views and experiences, and therefore diversity and difference is less likely to be problematised and more likely to be valued within a transformative model of higher education (Bamber *et al*, 1997, Jones and Thomas 2005). Tinto's work in the US has focused on the importance of academic and social interaction with the institution to improve student persistence (Tinto 1993). He found that students benefited from and enjoyed being part of 'learning communities', which forged interaction between students to facilitate their learning both inside the classroom and beyond (Tinto, 1998, 2000). Similarly Warren (2003) reviews existing literature (Liow, 1993; Husbands, 1996; Clarke, 1998; Sander *et al*, 2000) and finds that students prefer to be taught by group-based activities, particularly seminars, tutorials, group work and interactive lectures and feel that learning is fostered where activities, coupled with clear explanations, are experiential and practical.

Student-centred interactive learning does not only have to occur in small groups, but methods can be developed and utilised to teach large classes too. Warren (2003) identifies different methods that have been employed with large groups of students:

- collaborative learning groups (3–5 students) working on tasks during lecture periods (McKinney and Graham-Buxton, 1993);
- group presentations and interactive lectures featuring discussion of concepts and application to practical exercises (Prendergast, 1994);
- teaching via sessions that combine exposition and work on tasks in medium-sized groups (about 20 students), instead of whole class lectures (Goldfinch, 1996);
- resource-based learning in project study groups (6–10 students), culminating in a set of class debates to exchange knowledge gained (Sutcliffe *et al*, 1999).

(From Warren 2003, p4)

5. Providing intssegrated academic and pastoral support

There are different models of providing both academic and pastoral support. Warren 2002 identifies three ways of providing academic support: separate, semi-integrated and integrated curriculum models, and similarly Earwaker (1993) identifies traditional pastoral, professional and an integrated curriculum model as ways of providing both academic and pastoral support. Research on widening participation points towards the value of integrated models, particularly of academic support, with the provision of one-to-one support (Bamber and Tett, 2001; Comfort *et al*, 2002) and access to additional support as required (Comfort *et al*, 2002). Similarly, Warren argues that a mix of semi-integrated and integrated models of curriculum provision offers better prospects for helping a wide spectrum of students to succeed at university. Integrated approaches are favoured, as research shows that many students who would benefit from academic and other support services are reluctant to put themselves forward (Dodgson and Bolam, 2002), therefore a proactive or integrated approach helps to reach all students. Layer *et al* (2002) found that many HEIs with a commitment to wider access and above benchmark levels of retention have one-stop-shop student services. This type of provision not only makes it easier for students to access academic and pastoral services, but they encourage students to use the facilities by including services that all students may need to access and which are not stigmatising (e.g. accommodation office, sport and recreation, registry etc) (see Thomas *et al*, 2002a).

6. Alternative assessment strategies

Higher education research shows the benefits of formative as opposed to summative assessment for all students, as it supports them to 'learn how to learn' (Juwah *et al*, 2004). There has, however, been very little research explicitly linking formative assessment and widening participation – despite the seemingly obvious relationship (Thomas and Smith, 2005). A notable exception is George *et al* (2004), who argue that the combination of summative and formative assessment which was integrated into their curriculum design was 'critical to creating confidence, a positive attitude to education, and thence to successful engagement with cognitive demands' for disadvantaged adults on an Access programme. In particular they used facilitated self-assessment to support these students.

A second related area is the provision of alternative assessment opportunities, primarily for disabled students (Sharp and Earle, 2000; Heubeck and Latimer, 2002; Fuller *et al*, 2004; Riddell *et al*, 2004). The majority (with the exception of Sharp and Earle) support the need for alternative more suitable assessment strategies for disabled students – for example extra time, being able to stop the clock, sitting the assessment in a less intimidating setting. All students, particularly those coming from alternative educational backgrounds, could benefit from greater formative assessment and alternative assessment strategies.

How are institutions responding to widening participation?

Research literature suggests that institutions are not linking together widening participation and learning and teaching. For example, Layer *et al* (2002) found that only 37 per cent of institutions have addressed alternative ways to deliver the curriculum and only 3 per cent have addressed assessment. A recent UUK/SCOP study (Thomas *et al*, 2005a) explored the ways in which HEIs are addressing the widening participation agenda throughout the student life-cycle. A brief overview is provided here in relation to the six themes identified and discussed above.

1. Induction and the first-year experience

There is growing recognition across the sector of the need for effective transition strategies to support students to succeed in HE. Outreach activities are being used to prepare students for HE, rather than just increase rates of participation, and there are examples of extended induction programmes.

2. Introducing diversity into the curriculum

Curriculum development includes the creation of new 'products', such as Foundation Degrees, the introduction of new discipline areas and the development of the existing curriculum to create closer links between pre- and post-entry curricula. Curriculum innovations are more prevalent however in post-1992 institutions as opposed to pre-1992 universities.

3. 'Employability'

There are some examples of the integration of interventions designed to build commitment to the HE process as a means of achieving career goals, and equipping students with the skills to progress into employment or further learning on completion of their HE study being integrated into outreach and induction activities. Some institutions strongly promote work placements for their students. Students are also employed in widening participation initiatives, which assists them to develop transferable skills. In some institutions this learning is captured more formally than others.

4. Student-centred interactive learning

There is some recognition of the need to improve learning and teaching practices, and links between widening participation and learning and teaching staff have been developed, but this is not common. This is an important area for further development.

5. Providing integrated academic and pastoral support

Academic support is provided in both an integrated way (e.g. transferable learning skills modules and via PDP) and through separate drop-in facilities. Personal tutoring is being re-introduced in some institutions and becoming more structured so that both staff and students have a clear understanding about the purpose of sessions. Student services tend to rely on students accessing support, rather than a more proactive approach.

6. Alternative assessment strategies

Some institutions have reviewed either specific modules with high rates of failure or their whole curriculum to include additional assessment support and more formative assessment and feedback in the first semester.

In summary, the sector has received greater support to develop outreach and access interventions, and is very active and effective in this arena. This is now starting to influence interventions to support the transition into higher education, and thus institutions are revising their induction procedures, and in some cases their entire first-year experience. Learning and teaching developments in HE are in place in some institutions, but there is room for improvement – there are many areas where practices could be improved for the benefit of all students, but especially those from under-represented groups. In more traditional institutions, especially pre-1992 universities, there is a tendency to rely on the provision of additional learning support, rather than more embedded change. The more far reaching and challenging developments throughout the student lifecycle have been undertaken by some of the post-1992 institutions.

Conclusions: the future widening participation agenda

The research about widening participation and learning and teaching strongly suggest that institutional change is required to support the academic success of all students, and especially those from under-represented groups. The institutional research reported here (Thomas *et al*, 2005a), and previous studies (Woodrow *et al*, 1998: Layer *et al*, 2002; Woodrow *et al*, 2002), demonstrate that many institutions are not implementing far-reaching changes to their learning and teaching practices. This would appear to support the proposition that there is still strong support for a deficit model of widening participation, which requires students rather than institutions to change. Such an approach however ignores the many benefits of having a more diverse student body which can enhance the experience for all students and prepare them better for living and working in a diverse society.

The future widening participation agenda needs to focus on ensuring that the widening participation premium is used to create a transformative higher education sector, rather than to fund additional support interventions which reinforce an elite system. Furthermore, the current review of teaching funding in England provides an opportunity to influence learning and teaching in the future. Based on the review of literature and current practice, priority areas for the future widening participation agenda are:

- introducing diversity into the curriculum to enrich the learning experience of all students, and developing students' graduate attributes;
- mainstreaming interactive, student-centred learning and teaching strategies which are suitable for, and cost-effective in, the current HE system, across the sector;
- moving towards an integrated model of academic and pastoral support that enables all students to achieve their potential;
- reviewing assessment strategies that are suitable for all students, irrespective of their background, previous educational experience or disability (this could include a wider range of assessments and more formative feedback).

Note

1. The term 'success' is used here in preference to 'retention' as it suggests that not all students wish to complete their designated qualification within a proscribed time-frame. Success may be differently interpreted by individuals and groups of students. Recent research found that many young working

class students withdrawing from HE did not view the experience as 'failure'. UK policy, funding regimes and the media tend to conflate leaving early with failure (Quinn *et al*, 2005).

2. Paper cited with permission.

References

Askham, P (2004) 'The Feeling's Mutual: Excitement, dread and trust in adult learning and teaching', PhD Thesis, Sheffield Hallam University.

Avramidis, E and Skidmore, D (2004) 'Reappraising learning support in higher education', *Research into Post-compulsory Education*, 91.

Bamber, J and Tett, L (2001) 'Ensuring integrative learning experiences for non-traditional students in higher education', *Journal of Widening Participation and Lifelong Learning*, vol 31, 8-18.

Bamber, J, Tett, L, Hosie, E and Ducklin, A (1997) 'Resistance and determination: working class adults in higher education', *Research in Post-compulsory Education*, 21.

Barrie, S (2005) 'Starting the journey towards generic graduate attributes for a super-complex world', paper presented to the European Association for Research on Learning and Instruction 11th Biennial Conference, University of Cyprus, Nicosia, Cyprus, 23 –27 August 2005.

Blackwell, A, Bowes, L, Harvey, L, Hesketh, A J, Knight, P T (2001) 'Transforming work experience in higher education', *British Educational Research Journal*, vol 273, 269–85.

Bowl, M (2001) 'Experiencing the barriers: non-traditional students entering higher education', *Research papers in Education*, vol 162, 141–60.

Clarke, J A (1998) 'Students' perceptions of different tertiary learning environments', *Higher Education Research and Development*, vol 17(1), 107–17.

Clegg, S, Parr, S and Wan, S (2003) 'Racialising discourses in higher education', *Teaching in Higher Education*, 82,155–68.

Comfort, H *et al* (2002) 'A qualitative study investigating factors which help and hinder learning progression FE to HE', Report on the 'Transitions Project', Leicester: Leicester College.

Davies, P (1999) *Student retention in further education: a problem of quality or of student finance?* Further Education Development Agency http://www.leeds.ac.uk/educol/documents/00001257.doc

Dibben, N (2005) The influence of socio-economic background on student experience of teaching and learning in a British University Music Department, *British Journal of Music Education*, forthcoming.

Dodgson, R and Bolam, H (2002) *Student retention, support and widening participation in the north east of England* Universities for the North East http://www.unis4ne.ac.uk/unew/ProjectsAdditionalFiles/wp/Retention_report.pdf

Dogra, N, Conning, S, Gill, P, Spencer, J and Turner, M (2004) *The teaching of 'cultural diversity' in medical schools in the UK and Eire, British Medical Journal, vol 19;* 330 (7488): 4-3-4.

Earwaker, J (1992) Helping and supporting students, Buckingham: SKHE and Open University Press.

Evans, C (1990) 'Teaching the humanities: seminars as metalogues', *Studies in Higher Education*, vol 15(3), 287–97.

Foskett, N (2002) 'Marketing imperative or cultural challenge? Embedding widening participation in the further education sector', *Research into Post-compulsory Education*, vol 7(1).

Fuller, M, Healey, M, Bradley, A and Hall, T (2004) 'Barriers to learning: a systematic study of the experience of disabled students in one university', *Studies in Higher Education*, vol 29(3),303–18.

General Medical Council (1993) *Tomorrow's Doctors*, London: General Medical Council.

George, J, Cowan, J, Hewitt, L and Cannell, P (2004) '"Failure dances to the tune of insecurity"; affective issues in the assessment and evaluation of access learning', *Journal of Access Policy and Practice*, vol 1(2), 119–33.

Glover, D, Law, S and Youngman, A (2002) 'Graduateness and employability: student perceptions of the personal outcomes of university education', *Research in Post-compulsory Education*, vol 7(3), 293–306.

Goldfinch, J (1996) 'The effectiveness of school-type classes compared to the traditional lecture/tutorial method for teaching quantative methods to business students', *Studies in Higher Education*, vol 21(2), 207–20.

Haggis, T and Pouget, M (2002) 'Trying to be motivated: perspectives on learning from younger students accessing higher education', *Teaching in Higher Education*, vol 7(3) 323–36.

Hellmundt, S *et al* (1998) 'Enhancing intercultural communication among business communication students', *Higher Education Research and Development*, vol 17(3), 333–44.

Heubeck, B and Latimer, S (2002) 'Ability and achievement characteristics of Australian university students with self-reported specific learning disabilities', *Higher Education Research and Development*, vol 21(3), 273–87.

Hope, V and Sebastian, A (2000) 'Inclusivity workshops for first year engineering students', in L Thomas and M Cooper (eds) *Changing the Culture of the Campus: Towards an inclusive higher education*, Stoke-on-Trent: Staffordshire University Press.

Houghton, A-M and Ali, H (2000) 'Voices from the community: the challenge of creating a culturally relevant curriculum and inclusive learning environment', in A Jackson and D Jones (eds) *Researching Inclusion*. 30th Annual Conference, (3–5 July): 146–53, Standing Conference on University Teaching and Research in the Education of Adults (SCUTREA): Nottingham University.

Husbands, CT (1996) 'Variations in students' evaluations of teachers' lecturing and small-group teaching', *Studies in Higher Education*, vol 22, 187–206.

Jones, R (2006) Non-traditional student lifecycle in Jones, R and Jary, D (eds) *Widening Participation in Sociology, Anthropology and Politics*, Centre for Sociology, Anthropology and Politics, Higher Education Academy / University of Birmingham.

Jones, R and Thomas, L (2005) 'The 2003 UK government Higher Education White Paper: A critical assessment of its implications for the access and widening participation agenda', *Journal of Educational Policy*, vol 205, 615–30.

Juwah, C, Macfarlane-Dick, D, Matthew, B, Nicol, D, Ross, D and Smith, B (2004)

Enhancing Student Learning through Effective Formative Feedback, York: Higher Education Academy http://www.heacademy.ac.uk/senlef.htm .

Ko?ir, K and Peãjak, S (2005) 'The role of interpersonal relationships in students' learning engagement and achievement', paper presented to the *European Association for Research on Learning and Instruction 11th Biennial Conference,* University of Cyprus, Nicosia, Cyprus, 23–27 August 2005.

Laing, C and Robinson, A (2003) 'The withdrawal of non-traditional students: developing an explanatory model', *Journal of Further and Higher Education,* vol 27(2), 175–85.

Layer, G, Srivastava, A and Stuart, M (2002) 'Achieving student success', in *Student Success in Higher Education,* Bradford: Action on Access.

Leftwich, A (1987) 'Room for Manoeuvre: a report on experiments in alternative teaching and learning methods in politics', *Studies in Higher Education,* vol 12(3).

Liow, SR (1993) 'Course Design in Higher Education: a study of teaching methods and educational objectives', *Studies in Higher Education,* vol 18(1), 65–79.

Longden, B (2000) 'Élitism to inclusion – some developmental tensions', *Educational Studies,* vol 264, 455–74.

Marks, A (2000) 'Lifelong learning and the "Breadwinner Ideology": addressing the problems of lack of participation by adult, working-class males in higher education on Merseyside', *Educational Studies,* vol 263, 303–19.

Marks, A (2002) 'A "grown up" university? Towards a manifesto for lifelong learning', *Journal of Educational Policy,* vol 171, 1–11.

McKinney, K and Graham-Buxton, M (1993) 'The use of collaborative learning groups in the large class', *Teaching Sociology,* vol 21 (October), 403–8.

Murphy, M (2002) 'Creating new demand? The development of outreach access initiatives in higher education', *Research into Post Compulsory Education,* vol 7(3).

Parker, S, Naylor, P and Warmington, P (2005) Widening participation in higher education: What can we learn from the ideologies and practices of committed practitioners? *Journal of Access Policy and Practice,* vol 2(2), 140–60.

Preece, S and Godfrey, J (2004) 'Academic literacy practices and widening *participation: First year undergraduates on an academic writing programme',* Journal of Widening Participation and Lifelong Learning, vol 61, 6–14.

Prendergast, G (1994) 'Student centred learning in the large class setting', *Journal of Further and Higher Education,* vol 18(3).

Purcell, K, Morely, M and Rowley, G (2002) *Employers in the new graduate labour market: recruiting from a wider spectrum of graduates,* London: Council for Industry and Higher Education (CIHE) and Employment Studies Research Unit, University of the West of England.

Quinn, J, Thomas, L, Slack, K, Casey, L, Thexton, W and Noble, J (2005) *From life crisis to lifelon learning. Rethinking working-class 'drop out' from higher education,* York: Joseph Rowntree Foundation.

Ramsay, S *et al* (1999) Academic adjustment and learning processes: a comparison of international and local students in first-year university, *Higher Education Research and Development,* vol 18 (1), 129–44.

Rhodes, C and Nevill, A (2004) 'Academic and social integration in higher education: a survey of satisfaction and dissatisfaction within a first-year education studies cohort at a new university', *Journal of Further and Higher Education*, vol 28(2), 179–94.

Riddell, S, Tinklin, T and Wilson, A (2004) *Disabled Students and Multiple Policy Innovations in Higher Education* – Final Report, ESRC.

Sander, P *et al* (2000) 'University students' expectations of teaching', *Studies in Higher Education*, vol 25 (3), 309–23.

Sharp, K and Earle, S (2000) 'Assessment, disability and the problem of compensation', *Assessment and Evaluation in Higher Education*, vol 25(2), 191–9.

Sheppard, C and Gilbert, J (1991) 'Course design, teaching method and student epistemology', *Higher Education*, vol 22, 229–49.

Srivastava, A (2002) 'Good practice in staff development for the retention of students from groups under represented in higher education', *Journal of Widening Participation and Lifelong Learning*, vol 41, 14–21.

Sutcliffe, R *et al* (1999) 'Active learning in a large first year biology class: a collaborative resource-based study project on AIDS in "Science and Society", *Innovations in Education and Training International*, vol 36 (1), 53–64.

Thomas, L (2002) 'Student retention in higher education: The role of institutional habitus', *Journal of Education Policy*, vol 17(4), .423–32.

Thomas, L, Quinn, J, Slack, K and Casey, L (2002a) *Student Services: Effective approaches to retaining students in higher education*, Stoke-On-Trent: Institute for Access Studies (on behalf of Universities UK).

Thomas, L, May, H, Harrop, H, Houston, M, Knox, H, Lee, MF, Osborne, M, Pudner, H and Trotman, C (2005a) *From the margins to the mmainstram: embedding widening participation in higher education*, London: Universities UK and Standing Conference of Principals.

Thomas, L, May, H, Hatt, S and Elliott, T (2005b) 'Smoothing the transition', *Exchange Magazine*
http://www.heacademy.ac.uk/documents/Exchange_Issue_1.pdf

Thomas, L and Smith, B (2005) Using formative assessment to improve student retention, *Inclusion*. Issue no. 5 autumn, pp 24–9.

Thomas, L, Woodrow, M and Yorke, M (2002b) 'Access and Retention', in G Layer, *et al* (eds) *Student Success in Higher Education*, Bradford: Action on Access.

Tinklin, T, Riddell, S and Wilson, A (2004) 'Policy and provision for disabled students in higher education in Scotland and England: the current state of play', *Studies in Higher Education*, vol 29(5) 637–59.

Tinto, V (1993) *Leaving college: rethinking the causes and cures of student attrition*, Second Edition, Chicago: University of Chicago Press.

Tinto, V (1998) 'Learning communities and the reconstruction of remedial education in higher education', *Replacing Remediation in Higher Education Conference*, Stamford University, Jan 26–27.

Tinto, V (2000) 'Reconstructing the first year of college', in *Student Support Services Model Retention Strategies for Two-year Colleges*, Washington DC: Council for Opportunity in Education.

Wallace, J (2003) *Supporting the First Year Experience*, London Metropolitan University,
http://www.heacademy.ac.uk/embedded_object.asp?id=18998andprompt=
yesandfilename=CPD028 .

Warren, D (2002) 'Curriculum design in a context of widening participation in higher education', *Arts and Humanities in Higher Education*, vol 11, 85–9.

Warren, D (2003) 'Improving student retention: A team approach', Annual Conference of the Institute for Learning and Teaching in HE, University of Warwick, Coventry, 2–4 July.

Woodrow, M with Lee, M F, McGrane, J, Osborne, B, Pudner, H and Trotman, C (1998) *From Elitism to Inclusion: Good practice in widening access to higher education*, London: Universities UK.

Woodrow, M, Yorke, M, Lee, M F, McGrane, J, Osborne, B, Pudner, H and Trotman, C (2002) *Social class and participation: good practice in widening access to higher education*, London: Universities UK.

10

Widening participation – are academics signed up to the 50 per cent target?

Liz Allen

If we take widening participation as a given, then certain implications for staff flow from it – issues of changes to teaching and learning support, the curriculum, staff development, resources, staffing numbers, career progression and so on. But do we take it as a given – and, more to the point, do staff?

On a recent study trip to Illinois I was struck by the number of times that we were reminded that, in the US, everyone wants a college degree – even those who know they may never get one. It's not true in England, nor is the notion that it might be a perfectly legitimate aspiration for the large majority of the population. We still think a 50 per cent target is high – indeed some newspapers think it is risible.

With variable fees looming in English universities and colleges, to be closely followed by the outcomes of another round of research assessment, and with no sign of the traditional academic and institutional hierarchies being upset by these processes, perhaps the most critical question to ask about the relationship of academic staff to the widening participation agenda is – what do they think of it? Are people actually signed up to the 50 per cent target – and if so, on what terms? Even more critically, do institutional leaders know what their staff think?

I want to focus in this paper not so much on the more obvious implications for staff – for instance in terms of changing their teaching practice, changing the curriculum and reconsidering forms of support for students – but on this question of the underlying attitudes to the strategic objectives that policy-makers, and national agencies, already take for granted.

In my experience, in discussions with academics, and in particular with NATFHE members in the post-1992 universities and colleges of higher education (HE), certain themes emerge:

- commitment to the principle of open and equitable access to higher education and to diversifying further the mix of HE students;

coupled with four kinds of unhappiness:

- a very realistic linking of widening participation with low status in the league table and reputational pecking order;
- bitterness about exclusion from research and research funding, and a sense that the access mission is the institutional consolation prize;
- a sense of alienation from institutional strategic discussions;
- and nostalgia for the good old days.

Whilst union discussions perhaps tend to have a critical focus, it should be recognised that academic staff, and NATFHE members amongst them, contain many enthusiastic and positive proponents of widening participation. But, arguably, the widening participation project is at a stage where the shift needed is to move beyond the enthusiastic 'early adopters' to a more wholesale engagement of the majority of staff in institutions – very like the challenges facing the HE Academy in supporting institutions around changes to teaching and learning. An understanding and consideration of the underlying concerns and resistances amongst staff is crucial – as crucial as attention to specific resource and support needs. So – to expand on unhappiness, in reverse order:

The good old days

One popular formula for access to higher education is that it should be accessible (and free) to everyone capable of benefiting from it. What this actually means is contested territory amongst academic staff as much as anywhere else – as is the understanding of what 'it' is. So there are fundamental questions both about admissions, and about what students are admitted to. For many staff in the hardest-pressed departments in the hardest-pressed institutions, finance is perceived as driving admissions, just as it is feared that finance will increasingly drive decisions about student success and academic standards. The bottom line is the need to recruit students to courses.

The pressure on numbers, and the general pressures associated with expansion, are often confused with more focused issues of widening participation amongst specific target groups. Generalised anxieties about 'more means worse' crowd out the opportunities presented by 'different means better'. Staff may simply feel they no longer have the control they once had over admissions and academic standards, nor have had they had the opportunity to develop a positive consensus about new admissions policies and different expectations.

Questions about the ability of students to benefit from their HE courses are tangled up with pressures on resources, the ability and willingness of individuals to change their teaching and student support strategies, and the need for effective support from institutions for their staff as well as their students. But not only may staff have very real concerns about whether certain students have been appropriately admitted, they may not necessarily buy in to a 'mission' to teach those students who may have struggled hardest to get access to HE, be least well prepared for it and be the least obviously possessed of academic skills. It is probably true that, given the choice, as many academics in post-1992 institutions as in the research elite universities would choose academically-prepared, high-achieving and confident students if they could, however enthusiastically they might welcome greater diversity amongst such students. The reality, as many staff see it, is that in some cases the widening participation mission is not chosen but imposed. It may be worthy but not desirable.

At the same time whereas HE lecturers might be enthusiastic about expanding access and diversifying intake to the courses and curricula of *their* choice, they may be far more ambivalent about expansion based on developing qualifications, curricula, key skills and notions of employability that are rooted in a philosophy of a more vocationally-driven and student– demand-led HE. This is in part about the desire to offer non-traditional students the same HE that staff themselves had access to, on the same terms, rather than what is seen as a shorter, cheaper, more instrumental education. (The FE culture, of course, is different, with lecturers having different expectations about curriculum control and a different attitude towards vocationalism and employability – which in turn can provide more fertile ground for responsiveness to student demand.)

But issues of curriculum change also touch on the boundaries between academic autonomy, academic freedom – and academic control. One version of this is that the academic knows best what the student should want. It can also be understood as understandable defensiveness masking apprehension at the potentially transformative nature of widening participation – that new students will transform the 'academy' as much as they will be transformed by it.

Institutional strategy and planning

Another set of issues that can determine the relationship of academics to their institution's student intake – actual and aspirational – is the level of involvement they have in strategic planning, and in shared consideration of all the quality processes and academic procedures that underpin the student experience. For instance, institutional practice varied significantly in relation to the involvement of staff in drawing up access agreements with the Office of Fair Access (OFFA), and consulting over fee, bursary and scholarship support. Staff who will have in some sense to 'sell' courses to prospective students (and deal with the fall-out where they are dissatisfied) may have no input into institutional discussions about mission and pitch.

At the same time many academics are becoming increasingly anxious about the changing relationship of students to their education in the era of fees, and a customer-orientated culture. Caught, as it sometimes feels, in the middle, between student and institutional bureaucracy, academics express concerns both about the failure of systems to provide critical information about students – for instance in relation to student exclusions and the consequent impact on coursework and study – and the extent to which their employer will support them in questions of academic judgement and student complaints. There will be questions of dissent – differing views, for instance, about definitions of plagiarism, or appropriate student expectations with respect to support – but also lack of clarity about appropriate staff and student expectations, and about the procedures available to both. At both levels more needs to be done to ensure staff engagement and understanding.

The status of widening participation

The divisions and fault lines between institutions show up in relation to widening participation as they do in relation to all the other indicators – research, teaching, staffing and wealth. An analysis of the HEFCE performance indicators (Action on Access, 2004) shows the very clear institutional groupings in relation to intake and retention, which are mirrored by the nature of the tasks institutions have set themselves in their access agreements – to put it crudely, between making efforts to reach out to the very brightest of the working class, or to seek to support and retain an already diverse and less academically-well-prepared intake. Variable fees will add to the association between selectivity, the prestige of institutions and the academic attainment on entry of the students they admit. As now, students will themselves provide the academic cachet for their courses through their own prior attainment – the difference will be that they will then pay for it. Students will be prepared to pay higher fees to go to institutions that make it harder to get in.

Staff are acutely conscious of the place of their institutions in the various league tables – not only with respect to the nature of the access and retention mission, and the likely nature of the student intake, but with respect to the linkage of these with other aspects of institutional mission – not least, research. All the messages from the policy centre seem to suggest that diversification means choosing between research and teaching – for which read 'research and widening participation'. There is no doubt that across the HE sector, and within institutions themselves, work associated with widening participation carries relatively little status and reward, whilst research achievement continues to be the vehicle for peer esteem and career progression. For staff in the post-1992 colleges and universities, widening participation may seem to be the (underfunded) consolation prize for failing to succeed in the RAE.

And although 'underfunding' appears in parentheses above it is because of its predictability as an issue, not because of its relative unimportance. For academic staff in post-1992 institutions the funding of widening participation is already inextricably entwined with the funding of teaching and learning– because it impacts on most of their students and because retention strategies are likely to be embedded in the work done with all students.

Some solutions

There are plenty of positive and practical responses to the detail of concerns raised above. These might include:

- Staff and students, trade unions and institutional managements working together to ensure there is a solid, negotiated basis to procedures to support and help staff and students navigate the changing world (complaints, plagiarism, dealing with admissions, academic appeals) – coupled with discussion to achieve consensus about how they're to be used, and to reassure staff that their institution will support them as appropriate.
- Harmonising administrative and academic systems so that students can be supported in a timely way, and staff kept informed about issues to do with the students they teach. Exchange of information about student exclusions, for instance – and appropriate support on readmission. Timescales to allow staff to respond to student feedback, to review courses, and so on.
- Reward and career structures that value not only research, and teaching and learning, but also the full range of work associated with widening participation.
- Connections between different people and different activities within HE and across HE/FE (part of the idea behind the Action on Access Rough Guide).

- Developing the support and equitable employment of hourly-paid lecturers.
- Additional resources and time – for instance for academic advisers, tutors, and others for individual students.
- Using peer groups that are trusted and respected by staff – including the trade unions – to debate issues of widening participation.

But above all there are two underlying issues that are critical if widening participation is to be more enthusiastically embraced by a larger part of the academic community. One is the whole question of funding and the ways in which different elements of the funding of higher education do, and do not, interlink. The other issue relates to the terms of the academic debate around widening participation and what can be done to transform them.

I anticipate that other papers will be focusing on the funding issue – the context of variable fees, the need to address the funding of part-time students, the tensions with funding for research, the level of funding for teaching (and widening participation) and the potential changes to its methodology. We all know that if teaching and widening participation are not adequately funded then everyone is cynical about what is on offer and the extent to which access is opened up at the expense of choice.

What I want to conclude with are some observations on the terms of the debate around widening participation, and how it might appeal more – or differently – to a different and yet-to-be engaged group of staff. Widening participation – and teaching in higher education – is often described in ways that are worthy, deficit-driven and intertwined with the need for cost-reductions. To caricature (but only a bit): it is something we need to do, because it is socially just, because the economy needs more graduates, and because individual institutions are desperate for more students. However, it isn't accompanied by equivalent increases in funding, so it needs to be done more cheaply than in the past. And the students aren't as well prepared as students with high A-level scores, so they need additional support, if not remedial help.

How can we make the challenges of widening participation more academically stimulating than this? How can we think about celebrating diversity and see it as making teaching and research more exciting – rather than more onerous? In the final report of the Review of Fair Admissions, the Schwartz Committee noted that:

The presence of a range of experience in the laboratory or the seminar room enriches the learning environment for all students. A diverse student community is likely to enhance all students' skills of critical reasoning, teamwork and communication and produce graduates better able to contribute to a diverse society. The Group is aware of a recent decision by the US Supreme Court upholding a university's 'compelling interest in obtaining the educational benefits that flow from a diverse student body.' (Schwartz, 2004)

But the earlier summary of responses to the group's consultation also acknowledged that institutions may be positive about diversity in principle, but are far less clear about how to achieve it or how to maximise the benefits it could bring. Do we really think diversity is a good thing, or is it just hard work?

If we do (think it a good thing) then we need to apply that belief to the landscape of higher education as it is now, and to embrace actively all within higher education that is *not* the norm. This means, for instance, the part-time student, the part-time member of staff, the external professional experiences of teachers, the FE lecturers working on the first year of a franchised course, the non-academic experience of students, the different skills that students from different backgrounds bring with them – and their importance in any reconsideration not only of teaching and learning, but also of the curriculum and research contexts. Does working with different groups of students, and students from different communities, stimulate new reflection on subjects, on curriculum content, on research questions? How do we use those resources that we currently undervalue?

Part of the attempt to find new ways of talking about widening participation – ways that are academically interesting – must include the integration of thinking about research, and research strategies, with teaching and learning in the context of diversity. For those of us involved in the debate about the relationship between teaching and research, it is disappointing that HEFCE's description of its review of the funding method for teaching has nothing to say about its relationship with research. Whilst there is some debate in the sector about the ways in which synergy between research and teaching can be promoted and managed, and which considers scholarship and research other than that driven by 'RAE-able' publication, it is not often linked explicitly to the widening participation and diversity debate and *its* impact on learning and teaching.

Staff across all institutions want opportunities to engage in forms of research and scholarship and at the moment may see these as being in competition with the demands of widening participation and supporting student success amongst a larger and more diverse student group. Thinking on excellence in teaching and widening participation needs to be linked with opportunities for new kinds of thinking about research and used to offer new opportunities to staff and students alike. As well as embracing subject-based research, both pedagogic research and research into widening participation need to be developed, respected and supported – and the debate taken forward in an international context, starting at our own borders with more exchange between practitioners in England, Scotland, Wales and Ireland.

For those engaged in academic work across the spectrum, access and diversity must be at the heart of what makes academic life stimulating and challenging – not an irritant at the margins, nor an indicator of institutional low status. Alongside all the practical work and developmental support, staff and students need to re-engage in the debate about why we're widening participation and what everyone can get out of it.

References

Action on Access (2004) *Student Retention and HEFCE Performance Indicators*, London: Action on Access.

Schwartz, S (2004) *Fair Admissions to Higher Education: Recommendations for Good Practice*, Nottingham: DfES

11
HEIs and widening participation

Kevin Whitston

Widening participation is about social inequalities in access to higher education. It is fundamentally a problem of class and associated disadvantage: fair access addresses related inequalities and to make progress with either means raising attainment as well as aspirations, creating new higher learning opportunities as well as improving access to existing ones. In all of this HEIs have a profoundly important role to play: HEIs alone cannot widen participation but it cannot be done without them.

The data for widening participation are anything but encouraging. The proportion of students entering HE from state schools and colleges has inched upwards since 1998 (despite a small reverse in 2003–04) and the proportion coming from 'low-participation neighbourhoods' over the same period has moved from 12.3 per cent to 13.9 per cent. But the proportion of young first degree entrants from lower socio-economic groups remains unchanged. In these circumstances how do the basic propositions about widening participation stand up? And specifically what can be expected of HEIs in the period ahead?

To answer these questions we need a better understanding of what widening participation is, and is not, about.

Students from manual working-class backgrounds are not under-represented because HEIs are deliberately keeping them out. The *Times Higher Education Supplement* reported the findings of the National Audit Office (NAO) on widening participation under the headline, 'Institutions attacked for bias against poor'. But in fact the NAO found that the data they had were consistent, overall, with a lack of social class bias (National Audit Office, 2002: 9).

Nor are they under-represented because the academically qualified fail to apply. Five years ago it was common to suppose that widening participation was about encouraging HE entry among young people with good A-levels who might not otherwise go into HE. The need to raise aspirations was often framed in this way. In fact, few academically qualified youngsters fail to enter HE, and the differences in HE entry between socio-economic groups at any given level of academic attainment is small. Gorard argues that the 'qualified age participation index' is 100 per cent (Gorard, 2005: 13).The same is not true of those with vocational qualifications at Level 3. Fewer than half of those with vocational qualifications enter HE and among them, people from higher socio-economic groups are significantly more likely to do so than others (Haezewindt, 2004).

We will return to the position of learners on vocational routes. Leaving this matter to one side for the moment, the single most important reason for the under-representation of lower socio-economic groups is lower attainment. Three-quarters of children in 'higher professional' families achieve five or more GCSE grades A*–C compared with less than one-third from 'routine' occupational backgrounds. But this is no explanation at all. It begs the question why there should be such differences in attainment. The answer lies in class and associated relative disadvantage and this, though relatively familiar, needs spelling out before saying what we can reasonably expect HEIs to do about it.

In what follows it is argued that there has been progress in widening participation but in some ways the links between class, social disadvantage and educational attainment are closer and more influential than ever. This matters because educational inequalities are not an accidental by-product of social structures but are actively produced and reproduced. Cultural change accompanying mass higher education and new opportunities for vocational learners offer grounds for some optimism. But the influence of class and social disadvantage is at work here too. The commitment of HEIs to widening participation is a critical ingredient in a complex mix of social processes that determines whether the sector really does deliver for all those capable of benefiting from higher education.

Participation, class and social disadvantage

The participation rate in 2001 for those from non-manual backgrounds aged under 21 was 50 per cent, compared to 19 per cent for those from manual backgrounds. In the period since 1960 the participation of lower socio-economic groups increased at a faster rate, reducing their relative odds of entry compared to young people from more affluent backgrounds. But the figures grew from a very low base, so that the absolute increase in the numbers from non-manual backgrounds continues to put this progress in the shade.

A longitudinal study from the Office of National Statistics (ONS) shows how the 'long shadow of childhood' followed those surveyed into their adult lives. There was a degree of upward social mobility, with less movement down the social scale. The changing composition of the population benefited those from professional and managerial backgrounds. 'One reason for the continuing influence of parental occupation on the occupations of their children is the effect of family background on educational opportunity and attainment' (Buxton *et al*, 2005). Forty-three per cent of men from social classes 1 and 2 achieved HE qualifications compared with 14 per cent of those whose parents were in classes 4 and 5.

The narrative of social mobility is a familiar one. Absolute increases in mobility have little impact on the relative chances of those from different social groups. The change in the class structure creates room at the top:

> *But more room at the top has not been accompanied by greater equality in the opportunities to get there ... In sum, the growth of skilled white collar work has increased opportunities for mobility generally, but the distribution of those opportunities across the classes has remained the same*

> (Marshall, 1997: 5).

In fact, class, social mobility and educational attainment are now more intimately linked than ever so that 'class effects are increasingly being mediated through educational processes' (Savage, 2000: 90). Access to higher education is more important in reproducing the class structure.

Blanden et al (2005) show a link between parental income and educational outcomes and argue that social mobility measured by income groups was higher for those born in 1958 than for those born in 1970. However, the conclusion that higher education expansion in the 1990s benefited the rich far more than the poor is too simplistic. Machin (2003), too, argues that higher educational inequalities have grown but, as he acknowledges, the position of the middle income quintiles improved more than the top. And the rate of growth in participation (as opposed to the difference in percentage increases) was faster in the lowest quintile. We have to remember that this was a period of rising inequality. In the last twenty years of the old century the absolute income levels of the poorest 10 per cent remained unchanged while their share of income actually fell (Savage 2000, 45–6). Even glacially slow progress seems remarkable in the circumstances. Similarly Machin, using data from Glennerster (2001), finds no improvement for the lower social classes over the 1990s and points to the growing participation gap in percentage points between the classes. Again, a faster rate of growth has improved the relative position of those from lower socio-economic groups, even if this is from a low starting point. Glennerster's conclusion seems more appropriate:

social class access is influenced by 'the width of the gate through which applicants have to pass. The narrower the gate the more the middle class gain. The wider the gate relatively more working class students enter ... the expansion of the 1990s had a similar result despite the possible adverse effects of the changes in funding. This shows how important it is to keep the gate wide!'

(2001: 23).

Class and disadvantage distort the outcomes that ability might otherwise produce:

A number of studies, from different periods and places, have ... shown that even when ability is held constant, children are more likely to enter longer-term and more academic courses, the more advantaged the class origins from which they come.

(Goldthorpe, 1996: 496)

Class–related differences in education start early. By age 10 the child's socio-economic group can be a more powerful predictor of attainment than prior attainment, with low achievers from higher social backgrounds overtaking high achievers from lower social backgrounds (Feinstein, 2003). In the USA in 1992 the participation rate for low-income high achievers was roughly the same as that for high-income low achievers (Wolf, 2002: 195).

Inequality is not confined to processes culminating in access or exclusion. The question of 'fair access' refers to issues of equity for those who enter, or are on track to enter higher education. Academically able working-class youngsters do not end up in the most academically prestigious institutions in anything like the numbers they should. State school pupils at the same level of attainment are less likely to enter these institutions than pupils from the independent sector. There isn't an adequate explanation for this. No one suggests it is the result of bias in admissions but it happens anyway, perhaps reflecting the work yet to be done in changing expectations among learners and the accessibility and openness of institutions. There are related questions about ethnicity. Ethnic minorities are over-represented in higher education but concentrated in a narrow range of institutions. Gender raises other issues. In the 1950s only a quarter of HE students were female, today it is in excess of 50 per cent and there is evidence of a growing gap, with men falling behind rapidly.

There is often some impatience in the widening participation community with concerns about what the Sutton Trust has called the 'missing 3000', the students from under-represented groups who fail to enter the most academically prestigious institutions. This impatience is a mistake. There is no simple dividing line between social processes that produce unequal outcomes in educational attainment and those that produce other inequalities. It matters that students from state schools do not have the same opportunities as those from the independent sector. The latter continues to play a major role in reproducing social, economic and educational inequalities. Where gender and race are concerned the underlying issues are often ones of class. It is boys from disadvantaged neighbourhoods that are falling behind fastest (HEFCE, 2005), and as Halsey notes:

> *it may even turn out on further evidence that ethnicity per se is not a barrier: only the asymmetric fit of race to class produces apparent inequality of access, and the case for positive discrimination may be solely on behalf of the disadvantaged working class.*
>
> (Halsey, 1993: 131).

Inequality is not an accidental by-product of social structures. Outcomes are actively produced and reflect the competition for advantage between social groups. In educational terms, as the performance gap between social groups closes at one level it can open up at a higher level:

> *as those from the lower social classes have become more likely to achieve some qualifications, and more likely to stay on after 15 and 16, and so on, so their better-off peers have pulled ahead by achieving higher qualifications and, in particular, entering HE.*
>
> (Johnson, 2004: 187).

In the post war period the exclusion of working-class children was often attributed to the effects of selective schooling, lack of parental support, lack of familiarity with the opportunities of grammar school and university, and the preference for training and a trade. Middle-class families that had once paid for grammar school places now secured free places in competitive examinations. The essence of the system was selection, which established a hierarchy of schools 'with a major boarding school at the top and a "council school" at the bottom' (McKibbin, 1998: 271). Some of these influences are at work today. The HEFCE demonstrated the association between low participation on one hand and the experience of multiple disadvantage in areas of low participation on the other (HEFCE, 2005). Some children still do not have a quiet place to do homework. They may have hardly left the estate where they live, much less gone on trips to the theatre or on foreign holidays. And if they have loving and supportive parents they are not necessarily the parents who value educational success more highly than other kinds of achievement. They may be more concerned about their child's happiness than school success, and more inclined to accept both the school and their children's academic performance as a given (Carroll and Walford, 1997: Reay and Ball 1997).

Some old questions, still unresolved, appear in a new guise. Writers in the tradition of Halsey, Heath, and Ridge (1980) were critical of grammar schools as socially divisive and wasteful of the abilities of working-class children. Andrew Adonis (Adonis and Pollard, 1997), now a junior education minister, regrets their passing. Foundation schools, specialist schools, the extension of 'parental choice', and, most recently and most radically, academies, are breaking up the comprehensive system. There appear to be two aims: the desire to reconcile middle class opinion to state schools, and to reach unrealised potential among working class children. The 'gifted and talented' strand in the government's Excellence in Cities programme shares similar objectives. It identifies between 10 per cent and 20 per cent of the school population in large urban areas and focuses special efforts on raising their attainment. In some disadvantaged areas the gifted and talented programme has successfully engaged marginal learners and turned them on to academic achievement. The risk, of course, is that differentiated schooling, and programmes that divide children at age 14 into those who are gifted and talented and those who are not, will only confirm the status of the excluded majority. Gorard *et al* found that increased parental choice initially decreased the social segregation between schools but that the growth of selection since 1997 has reversed this trend (Gorard, Taylor and Fitz, 2003).

People working in widening participation need a sense of proportion. Their efforts are one contribution in a much larger social process. What happens in schools and families, in workplaces and communities, will have hugely significant effects. The truth is we are not always clear what those effects are. In his Colin Bell memorial lecture Howard Newby (2004) suggested that we know less today about the way educational attainment is socially produced than we did when Jackson and Marsden (1963) wrote about education and the working class. Class is a difficult category at the best of times and one that is only inadequately captured in data about occupations, even if the data were more discriminating and reliable than it actually is. It remains an indispensable concept, but the way we live now does not easily fit some of the categories we have inherited. In a period when economic restructuring is unsettling and recomposing classes, distinctions between manual and non-manual work don't mean what they once did. And if the association between disadvantage and educational attainment is intuitively obvious we don't know enough about how it works, about the inter- relationship of income, social class, and culture in the modern context.

We have probably not, for example, paid enough attention to the cultural shift that has emerged with mass higher education. The widening participation community often speaks as if we were in the 1960s, or even the 1940s. There are communities where people still think higher education is 'not for the likes of us' but this sounds more and more old-fashioned and out of joint. Young people talk about 'going to uni', or 'being at uni' in a way that would have been unthinkable even a generation ago. There is still some way to go but the cultural battle to strip 'uni' of its elevated and exclusive status as the 'academy' is being won. People don't 'go up' to 'read leisure and tourism'. This isn't to have a dig at academic excellence and certainly isn't intended to poke fun at leisure and tourism. Tourism probably employs more people world-wide than any other industry. And academic excellence in any field of study is still its own defence. It does mean that the language, form, and content of mass higher education are loosing their association with privilege.

Expectations are also beginning to change but there are significant constraints. Two thirds of 11–16 year olds in schools in England and Wales questioned by MORI survey for the Sutton Trust said they expected to go into higher education when they were old enough. One in three said they were very likely to do so. Such expectations are still structured by experience, in this case of differential schooling. Sixteen-year-olds attending 'Foundation schools' are significantly more likely than those from 'LEA schools' to say they are likely to go into higher education. Among eleven-year-olds, 87 per cent from grammar schools were likely to go, compared to 38 per cent from 'secondary schools' and 64 per cent from comprehensives. The degree of parental encouragement to enter HE follows the pattern of school-type, and parents are rated by young people as the most important source of information about this (Sutton Trust, 2002). Many children are receptive to HE. Many more would be so if the expectations of adults were more encouraging.

This raises other questions, posed most sharply by David Watson, in relation to the definition of under-representation: 'who is meant to be left out' (Watson, 2004)? Mass HE provides a new context for widening participation in more senses than one. As participation in higher education grows, the gap between those who can participate and those who cannot also grows. In a mass higher education system the significance of entry may not be so great but the cost of exclusion is higher. Widening participation into HE cannot just be about HE as it is now. Indeed, it must take account of the range of learning opportunities available to all, and the relationship between them.

What can we expect from HEIs?

What can HEIs do about any of this? Fair access is a minimum commitment. This isn't just about fair admissions. If HEIs want to recruit 'the best and the brightest' they will have to go out and get them. There should be no privileged stratum of institutions for a privileged group of students.

Can they do more? The deep social roots of the problem are no reason for those in HEIs to throw up their hands in despair and to look to 'society' or to schools to tackle it: the contrary is true. And that means all HEIs, not just those that recruit most intensively in disadvantaged communities. HEIs are deeply implicated in the way society reproduces itself, inequalities and all, and if they are part of the problem they have to be part of the solution. To their credit, few people in higher education have accepted the view that widening participation is entirely someone else's responsibility. It is not something HEIs can do on their own, but it won't be done without their wholehearted engagement.

And of course, the sector is already doing something about it, working with schools and colleges to raise aspirations and attainment with trips to university campuses, mentoring, student ambassadors in schools, and a host of related activities.

Some approaches need rethinking. We continue to speak about 'raising aspirations' and there are many contexts in which this is probably appropriate. On the other hand the term 'aspiration' carries a lot of middle-class baggage and some unfortunate moral undertones. It suggests that some youngsters (and/or their families) lack a strong enough desire to better themselves. Too little attention is paid to how aspirations are formed. Unless we are talking about fantasy, people aspire to things that are part of their universe, things that they expect to be possible not things that are impossible or irrelevant. It is more appropriate to think in terms of expectations than aspirations. Young people derive their expectations from parents, teachers, friends and experience generally. The possibility of higher education can become part of that experience and no one can communicate it more powerfully than those from HEIs.

HEIs can help raise attainment too, and must do so if expectations are not to be frustrated. They cannot substitute for what schools and colleges do, but properly integrated HEI input can bring something special. Occasional lectures, seminars, and workshops; student tutors working with small groups; assistance with sources, ideas and encouragement for projects; all these enrich learning, help motivate, and raise attainment. HE students gain invaluable experience, their institutions are more closely embedded in their communities, and the next generation of students are better prepared. There are striking examples of schemes of this sort in almost every town and city across the country.

The next step is to go beyond projects and initiatives to embed widening participation in the corporate policy and practice of all institutions. This is one of HEFCE's key priorities. Widening participation will not be achieved in the short term, and certainly not through a 'one off' adjustment. A commitment to widening access will take different forms in different institutions but as long as society generates inequality of access widening participation is part of the HE mission if higher education is true to itself.

Broadening opportunity as well as access

The sector can help open up new opportunities for new learners as well as improving access to what already exists. The post-Tomlinson 14–19 curriculum will have to offer something better than GCSEs and A-levels, enabling many more young people to register worthwhile achievements at school. Higher-level learning will need to adapt accordingly, developing curriculum content and delivery to meet the needs of vocational and academic learners, not just at the point when they leave school or college but across a working lifetime. Fewer young people with vocational Level 3 qualifications enter HE compared with those with academic qualifications, and too few subsequently find their way into HE as adults. When they do so they often find a sector that is not quite ready for them. We still have more than 60,000 graduates from HE Level 4/5 professional programmes in what is quaintly described as 'non-prescribed higher education'. Opportunities for further progression are circumscribed by the uncertain status of their learning and the variety of responses they are likely to encounter from one institution to another.

Lifelong learning networks that link colleges and HEIs will offer some progress here. They aim to provide the same clarity, coherence, and certainty for the vocational learner as exists for those on academic pathways. Networks should be established in every region before the end of 2006. As higher education develops its own skills strategy, and a lifelong learning strategy, it acknowledges the need to change to meet the needs of learners quite as much as learners need a certain level of achievement to access HE.

Broadening opportunity in this way is long overdue in higher education, as it is in schools. But it is not a substitute for continuing to challenge educational inequalities elsewhere. It remains just as important that working class scholars can pursue academic programmes and that they can access the most prestigious academic institutions as it is to ensure that apprentices can access higher level learning at all. Broader opportunity will not be achieved by creating a new kind of higher education for some while leaving the existing system to those who take most of the places in it now.

Unsurprisingly, the challenges of class and socio-economic disadvantage are a factor for vocational education and progression too. A higher proportion of those with Level 3 qualifications from manual backgrounds have vocational qualifications compared with those from higher socio-economic groups. Better progression opportunities for vocational learners should help tackle under-representation. However, while there are very small differences in terms of entry to HE between those from different social groups at any given level of academic attainment the differences are more significant for those with Level 3 vocational qualifications. Moreover 'twice the proportion of people from higher rather than lower social class backgrounds with a qualification lower than NVQ 2 entered HE by age 21' (Haezewindt, 2004: 17). Life was never simple.

Conclusion

Higher education will change significantly over the next decade, but some things should be non negotiable. The intellectual integrity of HE is one; a commitment to engage with society and to widen access should be another.

References

Adonis, A and Pollard, S (1997) *A class act: the myth of Britain's classless society*, London: Penguin.

Blanden, J, Gregg, P and Machin, S (2005) 'Social mobility in Britain: low and falling', *CentrePiece*, Spring.

Buxton, J, Clarke, L, Grundy, E and Marshall, C E (2005) 'The long shadow of childhood: associations between parental social class, educational attainment and timing of first birth; results from the ONS longitudinal study', *Population Trends*, Autumn 2005, 121 www.ons.gov.uk.

Carroll, S and Walford, G (1997) 'Parents responses to the school quasi-market', *Research Papers in Education*, vol 12(1), 3–26.

Feinstein, L (2003) 'Inequality in the early cognitive development of British children in the 1970 Cohort', *Economica*, vol 70, 73–97.

Glennerster, H (2001), 'United Kingdom Education 1997–2001', Centre for the Analysis of Social Exclusion, CASE Paper 50.

Goldthorpe, J H (1996) 'Class analysis and the reorientation of class theory: the case of persisting differentials in educational attainment', *British Journal of Sociology*, vol 47(3), 481–505.

Gorard, S (2005) 'Where shall we widen it?' *Higher Education Quarterly*, vol 59(1), 3–18.

Gorard, S, Taylor, C and Fitz, J (2003) *Schools, markets and choice policies*, London: RoutledgeFalmer.

Haezewindt, P (2004) 'Focus on social inequalities: education, training and skills', Department for Education and Skills, www.ons.gov.uk (Focus on inequalities).

Halsey, A H (1993) 'Trends in access and equity in higher education: Britain in international perspective', *Oxford Review of Education*, vol 19(2), 129–40.

Halsey, A H, Heath, A F and Ridge, J M (1980) *Origins and destinations: family, class, and education in modern Britain*, Oxford: Clarendon Press.

HEFCE (2005) *Young participation in higher education*, Bristol: HEFCE.

Jackson, B and Marsden, D (1963) *Education and the working class*, London: Routledge and Keegan Paul.

Johnson, P (2004) 'Education policy in England', *Oxford Review of Economic Policy*, vol 20(2), 173–97.

Machin, S (2003) 'Unto them that hath', *CentrePiece*, Winter.

Marshall, G (1997) *Repositioning class: social inequality in industrial societies*, Sage: London.

McKibbin, R (1998) *Classes and cultures: England 1918–1951*, Oxford: Oxford University Press.

National Audit Office (2002) *Widening participation in higher education in England*, London: HMSO.

Newby, H (2004) 'Doing widening participation: Social inequality and access to higher education', Colin Bell Memorial Lecture www.hefce.ac.uk.

Reay D and Ball, S J (1997) 'Spoilt for Choice: the working classes and educational markets', *Oxford Review of Education*, vol 23(1), 89–101.

Savage, M (2000) *Class analysis and social transformation* Buckingham, Open University Press.

The Sutton Trust (2002) 'School Omnibus 2001–2002: A Research Study among 11-16 year olds', MORI on behalf of the Sutton Trust.

Times Higher Education Supplement (18 January 2002) 'Institutions' bias against the poor'.

Watson, D (2005) 'Overview: telling the truth about widening participation', in G Layer (ed) *Closing the equity gap: the impact of widening participation strategies in the UK and the USA*, Leicester: NIACE.

Wolf, A (2002) *Does Education Matter? Myths about education and economic growth*, Penguin: London.

12

What I think I know and don't know about widening participation in HE

David Watson

I have been thinking about widening participation in universities and colleges around the world. This raises some big issues, including:

- normative questions about what institutions and the policy-makers responsible for them should be aiming for in this field;
- contextual questions about what aspects of the wider environment seem to facilitate or hinder such performance;
- empirical questions about how well national systems are meeting the challenge of equitable participation; and
- operational questions about how they could improve their performance.

To tip my hand at the beginning, some answers to these questions are highly culture-specific: to paraphrase John Kay on *The Truth about Markets*, higher education systems are 'culturally embedded'. Others raise issues which seem capable of generalisation across borders, and continents. These include the impact of:

- economic polarisation;
- social and ethnic discrimination;
- the expectations and performance of 'schooling' (or 'compulsory education'); and
- positioning in a global market for higher education and its services.

1 Normative questions: why should we widen participation?

The iron law seems to be that if you want higher education to be fairer, you have to allow it to expand. As you allow it to expand, you also have to consider the position of those who do not participate.

Figure 1 (after Martin Trow) shows how we used to look at expansion. It was devised in the context of a theory ('the Robbins Trap') that was actually about pulling up the ladder. Trow's advice to the UK was that if you let more people in you must reduce your ambition about the kind of experience they will have.

•	*elite* systems enrol up to 15 per cent of the age group
•	*mass* systems enrol 15–40 per cent of the age group
•	*universal* systems enrol more than 40 per cent of the age group

Figure 1: Trow's taxonomy
Source: Brennan, 2004

There are two problems here. The first is parochial: the 'Robbins trap' never in fact materialised in the UK, largely because of the performance of polytechnics, colleges, and subsequently the 'new new' universities. They have subsequently largely maintained their missions in respect of professional and vocational courses, service to local and regional communities, along with development of applied research, sometimes of real distinction (as in art and design) (see Watson and Bowden, 2002).

The second is universal and is contained in the data from the OECD in Figure 2. It is apparent that so-called 'elite' university education exists hardly anywhere in the world, and that most major systems are closing in on the 'universal' target. The global and historical truth about 'mass' higher education is that if you blinked you would have missed it. In response, Trow has moved the goalpost for 'universal' systems: it is now apparently 50 per cent (Trow, 2005).

Also bear in mind that this table is about 'completion' of first-level higher education, and not just – as in Trow's analysis – enrolments. As Thomas Weko has demonstrated, until very recently little attention was paid in the USA to 'completion' or its reciprocal, 'wastage' (legislators have been catching up fast). Weko's theory is that this is cultural: 'in the US view, completing a degree is better than not, *but something is better than nothing*' (emphasis in original) (Weko, 2004). In fact, evidence from the UK Wider Benefits of Learning Group (referred to below) would suggest that empirically this is not true: certain groups of students who drop out of HE fare worse than their peers who never start.

Figure 2: Ratio of tertiary graduates to the population at the typical age of graduation (2002) for all type A programmes (first time graduation) Source: Education at a glance - OECD Indicators 2004

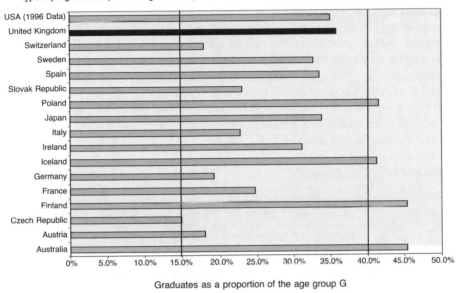

Graduates as a proportion of the age group G

Figure 2: OECD tertiary graduates

The more successful that national systems are in growing participation and achievement, the greater will be the gap between those who stay on a ladder of educational attainment and those who drop off. In the UK we have solid, longitudinal data about the positive effects of participation on not only the economic status of the individual beneficiary (in terms of HE the government's current almost-exclusive selling-point for its reforms), but also on their health and happiness and democratic engagement and tolerance, to say nothing of the life-chances of their children. I would refer you particularly to the output of the Wider Benefits of Learning Group at the Institute of Education (Bynner *et al*, 2003; Schuller *et al*, 2004).

We have a lot of international hand-wringing about 'completion,' 'persistence,' or 'retention' (as well as their reciprocals, 'drop-out' and 'wastage'). But the big picture is that we don't talk enough about 're-starting' or 're-engagement.' The most important issue is the growing gulf between a successful majority and a disengaged minority. The permanently disengaged become the individual 'self-blamers' whose histories have been eloquently mapped by Karen Evans and others (Evans, 2003); collectively they make up what Ferdinand Mount calls the newly discovered class of 'downers' (Mount, 2004).

There are serious issues for social mobility. Is HE simply a sorting device or does it have transformative possibilities? Unless it begins to deliver the latter, its social effects will be regressive. There is already evidence from high-participation societies that the effect on inter-generational mobility is negative (see the table below, derived by the Sutton Trust from a series of national cohort studies: the correlation is with inter-generational status persistence, so the higher the figure in the right-hand cell the lower the mobility (Blanden *et al*, 2005: 6)). This echoes an earlier conclusion from the Number 10 policy unit that the principal effect of the UK's expansion has been to prevent downward social mobility for 'dull middle class children' (PIU, 2001).

Country	Dataset	Sons Born	Intergenerational partial correlation
Britain	British Cohort Study	1970	.271
USA	Panel Study of Income Dynamics	1954–1970	.289
West Germany	Socio-Economic Panel	1960-1973	.171
Canada	Intergenerational Income Data (from tax registers)	1967-1970	.143
Norway	Register data	1958	.139
Denmark	Register data	1958-1960	.143
Sweden	Register data	1962	.143
Finland	Quinquennial census panel	1958-1960	.147

Figure 3: Internationally comparable estimates of intergenerational mobility

2 Contextual questions: what are the key cultural influences?

The English Higher Education Act of 2004 put the concept of 'under-represented groups' on the face of legislation (I believe) for the first time. While undoubtedly well-meaning, this may turn out to be a dangerous development. The notion of a political majority determining who is and who is not 'under-represented' at any time should chill the blood.

A survey of the fate of what might be regarded as 'under-represented groups' around the world will show what I mean. Turn the question on its head, and look at local cultural and political hang-ups. Who, in fact, is meant to be left outside?

Let me refer you to several controversies in contemporary international higher education which have the common feature of protecting majorities against minorities (see Beth McMurtie in the *Chronicle of Higher Education* (hereafter *CHE*), 13 February 2004).

- In China, in contrast to the admission advantage given to speakers of 55 minority languages, there was until very recently official discrimination against students with physical disabilities (see Jiang Zuequin in *CHE*, 26 July 2004); until 2001 the national college entrance exam was barred to students over 21 or married (Duan, 2003).
- British universities know that in large part their success in recruiting from Pacific Rim countries arises from the legal preference given to indigenous groups which causes a disproportionate number of the Chinese minority to seek their HE overseas.
- In Israel there has been a political U-turn over entrance tests, as their abandonment has apparently not advantaged working-class Jews but Arab-Israelis instead (see Haim Watzman in the *CHE*, 26 March 2004, and Chris McGreal in *The Guardian*, 1 December 2003).
- In Hungary, at the moment of accession to the EU, only 0.22 per cent of the country's Gypsies get as far as college (see Colin Woodard in the *CHE*, 19 March 2004).
- In Japan Wako University has revoked its offer of admission to the daughter of the leader of the Aum Shinriko sect (the perpetrator of the 1995 Sarin gas attack). She and her siblings have renounced the sect, but, in the words of the President 'she is likely to prompt uneasiness' and 'there may also be criticism from society' (see Alan Brender in the *CHE*, 22 April 2004).
- Brazil has just opened its first university with a 50 per cent quota for black students (see Marion Lloyd in *CHE*, 29 October 2004).

These snapshots also raise the question of differential public confidence in national university systems. To put the point plainly, some societies like their universities more than others (contrast, for example the United States and Australia). This is another potential problem that will only be overcome by expansion and widened participation.

More generally, in any society at any point in time there may be consensus about who the 'under-represented' groups are, but it is surely a dangerous hostage to political fashion; in the UK, for example, 'degrees for votes' could perhaps follow in the footsteps of 'homes for votes.'

Meanwhile, some of the messages are difficult: probably the UK group which is most under-represented statistically (and most frequently forgotten) is that of children formerly in care (Jackson _et al_, 2005).

The basic point is that widening participation is not just about minorities. The equation of (class) x (gender) x (ethnicity) x (age) x (location) is a very complex one. In the United States and the UK, for example, the position of poor young white males is now recognised as one of the most intractable problems (Jones, 2005).

3 Empirical questions: how are we doing?

International benchmarking is notoriously difficult in this, as in many other, educational settings. I would like to take the opportunity to introduce a dimension we rarely tackle, which is a comparison of participation indices across the European Union. The data (analysed by Brian Ramsden) are based upon a study called 'EuroStudent 2000,' which the UK government declined the opportunity to join (Slowey and Watson, 2003: 3–19).

It is interesting to note that, compared to the rest of the (current) EU, we in the UK have:

- the highest proportion of part-time students;
- the highest average age of participants;
- the highest proportion with disabilities (although classification is notoriously difficult here);
- the second-highest rate of working-class participation (behind Finland, one of the most 'planned systems' in the EU);
- the lowest rate of 'study from home,' and
- the second lowest 'regional' effect of recruitment.

It is interesting to reflect on how this pattern may be changed by the 'accession' states (and some useful preliminary work has been done by the Higher Education Policy Institute (HEPI, 2004)). I anticipate not much. In the meantime, it is worth reflecting on why (despite all of our legitimate concerns about equity) the UK seems to do comparatively well. Looking from the United States to the UK, the latter may seem less diverse and more fixed into a traditional mould. Looking from the UK to Europe puts everything in an entirely different light.

Can we use this insight to begin to categorise whole systems? Such categorisation usually proceeds from three starting-points: the 'market' model (where the customer rules); the 'corporatist' model (where the institutions are governed, formally and informally by a variety of stakeholders, public and private); and the 'state' model (where institutions are in effect instruments of national political will). These are, of course, ideal-types, and most systems will have mixed elements. Hans Schuetze and Maria Slowey have suggested a polarity between a highly traditional Continental model and a more flexible and relatively responsive approach in the more recently 'massified' English-speaking world. That has not prevented the further entrenchment in these countries (the USA, the UK and Australasia) of institutional hierarchies which themselves push significant commitments to the process of widening participation into lower-status institutions (see Schuetze and Slowey, 2000: 23; Slowey and Watson, 2003: xxiii–xiv).

Another way of tackling this differentiation is to look at how 'age-bound' different systems are. Tom Schuller and his group within the OECD have focused in particular on the fate of adult learners in tertiary education (Schuller, 2005).

A further question – to which I shall return right at the end (because I don't know the answer) – is whether or not the rapid development of 'borderless provision' renders some of these questions obsolete?

4 Operational questions: what works?

Widening participation is another field that has not fully absorbed the difference between policy-learning and policy-borrowing, and this has huge effects upon practice.

Another candidate for a universal truth is that institutions almost everywhere will admit the students which it is easiest and most profitable to recruit and then go looking for the rest. This is true within as well as between universities, to an extent that it will hardly be touched by the mild meliorism of the UK Schwartz Commission (DfES, 2004). Another hazard is the UK's rose-tinted view of 'needs-blind' selection by American elite universities, as recent muck-raking volumes attest. These include James Steinberg's *The Gatekeepers: inside the admissions process of a premier college*, on Wesleyan, and Christopher Avery, Andrew Fairbanks and Richard Zeckhauser's *The Early Admissions Game* on Harvard (see also the article by Louis Menand in *The New Yorker*, 7 April 2003, 'The Thin Envelope'). More recently William Bowen (President of the Mellon Foundation) and his collaborators have identified how 'merit aid' is channelled to students who do not really need it, and to athletes whose use of it is anything but academic (Bowen *et al*, 2005).

There are two other Trow traps here. First, that you can do it on the cheap, as with the enthusiasm – shared by many within the UK – for short-cycle HE in FE institutions. The Scottish data should give us real pause here: HE in FE in Scotland (proud as Scotland is it is of its superior participation rate) has led to under-funding, incompletion, and demonstrable lack of fairness in progression (Field, 2005: 127–35). Secondly, the California State system hardly remains a model. Here we have the header tank theory applying in spades: as the state budget has been squeezed, the equity commitments in the Master Plan have fallen by the wayside. David Kirp has recently reported that for Spring 2004 entry the University of California returned 2,000 transfer applications unread, while the California State system rejected 30,000 qualified applicants for transfer (Kirp, 2004).

A question which elides the empirical and the normative is that of *ambition*. By international standards the UK is doing well at some extremely important aspects of HE (research, retention, the global market, and so on). We are also doing well at lifelong learning (including CPD) for those members of society who remain engaged. We are doing less well in the immediate post-compulsory area, and this is where the fork in the road between the engaged and the disengaged appears to be located.

This is largely because of where this particular sector starts in the UK: at 16 formally, and at about 14 informally with the increasing evidence of disaffection in schools. What we know is that the 'participation gain' generated by the much-needed form of the 16+ examination system is probably now exhausted (Aston, 2003). Figure 4 gives the stark comparative picture. It is easy in this context, to labour to produce a mouse (as has the HEFCE with its massive report on *Young Participation in Higher Education* (January 2003: Report 2005/03)): we know that HE life-chances are set well before presentation for matriculation is a question.

But we also have to return to the cultural questions. What are the implications of wanting to look like, for example:

- Singapore – a society constructed around success in very traditional public examinations;
- or the United States – with its huge Community College network;
- or Australia – with its centrally-driven TAFE system (essentially a 'national curriculum' for vocational learning);
- or New Zealand with its universal 'tertiary entitlement;'
- or Germany – where contrary to many people's belief, students now regularly use intermediate level vocational qualifications to re-enter 'academic' or general higher education?

Figure 5 is an 'ambition' reality check, about the qualifications and commitment of managers in some of these societies. If this is a measure of capacity at the top of the pyramid, it's worth thinking about the relative expectations each group here has of those who work for them.

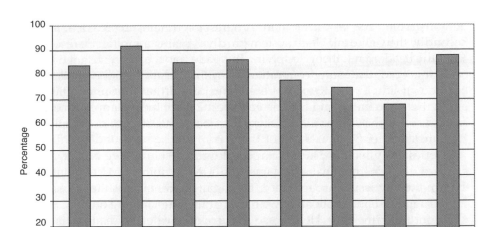

Figure 4: Population aged 25–34 with at least upper secondary education (HS graduate) 2001

	UK	USA	Japan	Germany	France
Average terminal education age (1999, years)	19.5	22	21	21	22
Graduate (%)	49	74	78	72	61
Days off-the-job training (1998)	4	7	5.5	5.5	6
Days on-the-job training (1998)	4.5	8	6.5	6.5	6
Source: Keep and Westwood, 2002 (in CIHE, 2004)					

Figure 5: Education and training of British management

5 Conclusions: what I think I know and don't know about widening participation

Putting this all together simply confirms how hard it is to know exactly *what* to do and *how* to do it. I think I'm much clearer on the *why* questions.

I think I know, first up, that if you want a fairer system in almost every case you have to allow it to expand (see Watson and Taylor, 1998:

27). Expansion has produced more equal opportunities for women, for minorities (in general), for those with disabilities, for older learners (including those returning to learn). But expansion costs: you have to 'ride the tiger,' and hope that resources will catch up. I've also learned that expansion, by itself, will not help (and can hinder) social mobility.

This leads to the second big lesson: that, the more the system expands, the greater will be the cost of not participating and, except in unusual circumstances (for example, all of those computer games undergraduates at Abertay who are lured into employment before they can graduate) of dropping out (even the games millionaires may live to regret it). Hence the key issues are retention, re-engagement, and risk (and, as I have suggested, internationally we have focused much more on the first than on the latter two). Hence also the importance of access to something worthwhile, so that HE remains part of the solution to social polarisation and not just a further exemplification of the problem (see Brennan *et al*, 2003). Hence the need to keep quality within an acceptable range; and hence also the crime of over-selling (and I'm serious about using such an extreme descriptor).

Third, and without in any way diminishing higher education's role in such 'solutions', success in compulsory education is vital. What is more, you don't get this by separating sheep from goats, whether or not the pens are labelled 'academic' and 'vocational' or 'public' and 'private.' This goes to the heart of national ambition, and I think that the UK is seriously wanting in this respect, including most recently in the political response to the Tomlinson Report.

Essentially we have created a fault-line between success and failure post-sixteen because we are scared of the alternative: that of declaring that nobody's publicly-supported education and training should cease at sixteen. In most other advanced economies this is not only unthinkable, it's also illegal. In her 1997 report *Learning* Works, Helena Kennedy was adamant that the threshold level for subsequent happier and more productive lives stands at Level 3, not Level 2. If we want a high-added-value, knowledge-based, globally competitive economy, we should understand that it is incompatible with maintaining what is called 'the youth labour market.' HE can't tackle this problem by itself; equally it can't simply say that it's somebody else's job. In the words of one of my colleagues at the University of Brighton, we have to get beyond the idea that 'outreach involves a direct "sell" of the benefits of HE'. It has to be much more than that.

Fourth, and finally, we must accept (and respond to) the fact that institutions can be hard-wired to resist this agenda. I've discussed already the 'header tank' on admissions. I haven't talked about our reluctance, inside universities and colleges, to lead the relevant public policy debate. (What's more, it is yet another set of priorities that institutional leaders seem to discover when they are about to retire.)

As for what I don't know, much of it is about how to make all of this happen (and some of what follows will sound a little despairing).

I don't know how most effectively to tackle the question of public confidence (except by waiting for improved participation rates to do it for us: what F. M. Cornford called 'the effluxion of time'). A new generation of staff may help here (see HEFCE Report 2005/23, Figure 8).

To take an instrument that is in our hands, I don't know what to do about the practice (as opposed to the theory) of credit accumulation and transfer. Simply declaring credit ratings will achieve nothing unless and until many more institutions (including those perceived as the most prestigious) are prepared to enable the owners of credits to cash them in.

And I don't know what the long-term effects of both new forms of provision and an inevitable de-regulation (perhaps coupled with anticipatory piracy) of borderless provision is going to be. I am buoyed by the historical example of the UK Open University: perhaps the best-worked example of educational innovation and social emancipation around the world since the London external degree.

I do know that cross-border innovation won't be a panacea. I'd like to know what you think could be.

Note

Parts of this paper are based upon the author's chapter 'Overview: telling the truth about widening participation' in Layer (ed.), *Closing the Equity Gap: the impact of widening participation strategies in the UK and USA* (Leicester: NIACE, 2005), 33–50, as well as a presentation to the FACE Annual Conference *Towards a Global of Understanding of Lifelong Learning* on 8 July 2005

References

Blanden, J, Gregg, P and Machin, S (2005) *Intergenerational Mobility in Europe and North America*, London: The Sutton Trust (April).

Bowen, W G, Kurzweilk, M A and Tobin, E M (2005) *Equity and Excellence in American Higher Education*, University of Virginia Press.

Brennan, J and Shah, T (2003) *Access to What? Converting educational opportunity into employment opportunity*, CHERI: London, December.

Brennan, J (2004) 'The Social Role of the Contemporary University; contradictions, boundaries and change', in *Ten Years On: changing higher education in a changing world*, London: CHERI (Centre for Higher Education Research and Information), 22–6.

Bynner, J, Dolton, P, Feinstein L, Makepiece, G, Malmberg, L and Woods, L (2003) 'Revisiting the benefits of higher education: a report by the Bedford Group for Lifecourse and Statistical Studies', Bristol: Institute of Education, HEFCE (April).

CIHE (Council for Industry and Higher Education) (2004) 'Solving the skills gap', Summary Report from a AIM/CIHE Management Research Forum, London: CIHE.

DfES (Department for Education and Skills) (2004) *Fair admissions to higher education: draft recommendations for consultation*, DfES/Admissions to Higher Education Steering Group, April.

Duan, X-R (2003) 'Chinese higher education enters a new era,' *Academe*, 4 December.

Evans, K (2003) 'Learning for a living? The powerful, the dispossessed, and the learning revolution', University of London, Institute of Education professorial lecture, 19 February.

Field, J (2005) 'Widening access and diversity of provision: the expansion of short-cycle higher education in non-university settings', in G Layer (ed) *Closing the Equity Gap: the impact of widening participation strategies in the UK and USA*, Leicester: NIACE, 124–40.

HEPI (Higher Education Policy Institute) (2003) *Projecting Demand for UK Higher Education from the Accession Countries*, HEPI Report Summary 8: Oxford, March.

Jackson, S, Ajayi, S and Quigley, M (2005) *Going to University from Care*, London: Institute of Education.

Jones, R A (2005) 'Where the boys aren't', *Crosstalk*, 13(12) (Spring).

Kay, J (2003) *The Truth about Markets: their genius, their limits, their follies*, London: Allen Lane. .

Kirp, D L (2004) 'Access denied', *National Crosstalk* 12(1) (Winter), 11–12. Mount, F (2004) *Mind the Gap: the new class divide in Britain*, London: Short Books.

PIU (Performance and Innovation Unit) (2001) *Social Mobility: a discussion paper*, London: PIU.

Schuetze, H G and Slowey, M (2000) *Higher Education and Lifelong Learners: international perspectives on change*, London and New York: Routledge Falmer.

Schuller, T (2005) *Learning from Each Other: Angles on institutional research*, Presentation for NIACE/OECD conference on 'Learning, Participation and Policy,' London, 9 May.

Schuller, T, Preston, J, Hammond, C, Brassett-Grundy, A and Bynner, J (2004) *The Benefits of Learning: the impact of education on health, family life and social capital*, London: Routledge Falmer. .

Slowey, M and Watson, D (2003) *Higher Education and the Lifecourse*, Maidenhead: SRHE and Open University Press. .

Trow, M (1989) 'The Robbins Trap: British attitudes and the limits of expansion', *Higher Education Quarterly*, 41:3, 268-92. .

Trow, M (2005) 'Reflections on the transition from elite to mass to universal access: forms and phases of higher education in modern societies since WWII', forthcoming in P Altbach (ed) *International Handbook of Higher Education*, New York: Kluwer.

Watson, D and Bowden, R (2002) *The New University Decade, 1992–2002*, University of Brighton Education Research Centre Occasional Paper (September). .

Watson, D and Taylor, R (1998) *Lifelong Learning and the University: a post-Dearing agenda*, London: Falmer Press.

Weko, T (2004) *New Dogs and Old Tricks: what can the UK teach the US about university education?* Mimeo, March

13

End Note – progress, perceptions, prospects

Chris Duke

The papers which were the basis for the chapters in this book, with one added later to provide a perspective from the English Higher Education Funding Council, were brought together in their initial form for a one-day discussion by twenty invited people in July 2005. Clusters of papers were briefly introduced to stimulate open and iterative consideration of the central themes. Between them, the symposium members represented most of the main 'stakeholder perspectives' on widening participation (W/P) into higher education in England. The papers were revised to varying degrees in light of that interaction, and are brought together in this volume. This concluding note seeks to convey something of the tenor of discussion.

The mood of the meeting in part reflected its timing. Was this a critical moment, a turning point in the long march towards a more open and accessible higher education (HE) system? And if so, a turn in which direction? It was recognised that we had moved in barely half a lifetime from a small elite system to one characterised in the literature as 'universal' rather than merely 'mass', yet a system which perpetuated strong hierarchy and privilege, legitimated as diversity. The work of Action on Access for the earlier Partnerships for Progression (P4P) and of Aimhigher, sponsored and supported by the Higher Education Funding Council for England (HEFCE), is unusual by international standards. It is of interest to system managers and widening participation (W/P) practitioners in other countries, as a series of comparative international studies carried out by Action on Access during the year and supported by HEFCE has shown. W/P remains one of the core purposes and strategic priorities of HEFCE as the Council rolls its strategic plan forward.

However, several relevant changes have yet to impact on the system and its W/P. Variable or 'top-up' fees are about to come into effect – with very little variability other than possibly in the further education (FE) sector, where part of the growth of HE is being channelled in the form of short cycle (two-year full-time or equivalent) foundations degrees FDs). In almost all cases variability proves to mean £3,000 a year, with different forms of discounting, scholarships, bonuses and come-ons to nurture the recruitment of high-scoring students from poor backgrounds in so-called selecting universities, and of larger numbers of those traditionally excluded from higher education in universities having a strong access mission. As we go to press, campaigns are running to tell prospective students how the Australian-style deferral of payment can be managed; it is hoped that as with the Australian Higher Education Contribution Scheme (HECS) a combined fees and loans regime will not deter, in particular, working class students.

Then there was the Schwartz review, generally felt to be a disappointment; the Tomlinson review, widely very well received, and emphatically judged by most to have been a bad lost opportunity; the ending of institutional access agreements with HEFCE; and the new system of agreements required by the Office for Fair Access (OFFA) before institutions can actually charge the new 'variable' fees. OFFA too was seen within this gathering as not so much a lost opportunity as an all-but-toothless compromise.

Slightly further out there will be the change of admissions procedures to what is called PQA – post-qualifications admission – long held to be impossible despite its long-established normality for example in Australia. PQA is officially heralded as likely to widen participation, since this clientele tends to score better at Advanced Levels than predicted. It remains to be seen whether there are other, unintended, consequences; and whether the powerful present emphasis on 'fairness' rather than equity (much less affirmative action or positive discrimination) might not lead to a more restrictive and mechanistic reliance on grade scores.

In the shadows behind these visible changes there was and is a debate of what has come to be called the dog whistle kind, about quality and standards. This latches on to wastage or drop-out as a whipping boy, despite remarkably low UK levels of withdrawal and non-completion, to say that expansion is not what the country needs, that the 50 per cent target is too high, or indeed that no target is needed and that the market should decide, and allow the system should contract. This is the position of the main national opposition political party, even though the target has been increasingly softened and is modest by comparison with the significant number of OECD states already well above fifty per cent. At one moment the meeting felt itself to be looking towards a system that would be more integrated and better planned to deliver its objectives and outcomes; in the next the mood was one of lost opportunity, especially compared with devolved Scotland which has moved more decisively to more integrated planning and now funding of a larger *de facto* tertiary system.

Planning is all very well, but what is really working, and what can really work in the tradition and policy environment that we have? It was suggested that a bicycle is only a bike if you can actually ride it, and that this applied to credit accumulation and transfer systems that are perfectly well created, but seldom result in recognition of previous study accredited, when this accreditation is taken forward for use in entering another institution or course at an appropriate level. It is being recognised within the OECD that this failure of working recognition and granting of advanced standing could be of interest to Treasuries, representing as it does a substantial waste of educational assets, in unnecessarily lengthening courses, and high opportunity costs for the individuals involved. All in all, the discussions suggested that England is overly reliant on swapping 'good practice', while policy and its outcomes are seriously under-examined. The policy environment is also seriously overheated politically: gleefully ferocious elements in the media have tended to make government risk-averse, at a cost to the kinds of innovation that are likely to widen access.

In short, the mood of the meeting, despite a wish perhaps to celebrate the approaching completion of a second three-year cycle of Action on Access work in support of widening participation by institutions, was less than sanguine, sending out a clear warning against complacency: like democracy, access and equity have constantly to be renewed and rediscovered if they are not to be eroded away.

That said, as the final main paper in the symposium and in this volume shows, the UK including England does remarkably well on some key performance indicators, especially by comparison with continental Europe, though less so when compared within the old Commonwealth and 'Anglo-Saxon' world. This shows up, for example, in the proportions studying part-time. Yet inaccessibility and inequality of opportunity remain highly intransigent. They are open to amelioration in practice, it seems, and as David Watson points out, only by continuing system growth. This means riding the tiger: in turn it creates other problems, among them obviously cost, but also because it touches the raw nerves of protectionist conservatism that will not willingly tolerate anything more than or different from an expanded elite system.

From a broader perspective, as Bob Fryer indicates, there is still further to go if we are to achieve the aspirations of a 'new economy knowledge society' in which lifelong learning is more than a slogan. There has been no progress to speak of in opening out higher education to recognise, accredit and embrace learning through and on the job. The time-honoured academic–vocational divide still has life in it, and learning other than from a regular academic institution base counts for little. The function of HE as a social selector allocating life-chances remains a powerful barrier to W/P – you only succeed competitively to the extent that others continue to fail.

One way to summarise the findings of the symposium (without detracting from the more rich and informed consideration of the different elements and players contained in earlier chapters) is to ask about failed or missed opportunities, and stalled or precarious progress.

In the first category would belong both the Schwartz and the Tomlinson reviews and reports, mentioned earlier: the one in how modest was the change proposed and carried out; the other in that far-reaching yet sensible and practicable changes were indeed proposed but promptly set aside by the newly appointed Minister of Education. Whereas W/P, in its admissions aspect as distinct from the student experience and retention following admission, is centrally about 14–19, and even younger, learning experience and aspiration-raising, it was made evident that there is still no clear, integrative 14–19 policy ambition, and no political will to bring vocational secondary-level education closer to parity.

Another area most honoured in the breach, for all the good words, is information, advice and guidance (IAG). And another, already referred to above, is articulation and progression between courses and kinds of courses, as well as institutions. The accreditation of prior experiential learning (APEL) can be added to the list, and within this the particular – politically most significant – element of work-based and workplace learning. More broadly, vocational education remains relatively under-valued, under-funded and frequently stigmatised.

At a local and regional level partnership and place are still not strong. Policy and institutional efforts are highly focused on the individual student in their aspirations, approaches and measures, rather than adopting a neighbourhood or regional strategy. (It remains to be seen whether this will change if Aimhigher-type initiatives lead to deep and sustained partnerships with schools, largely on a regional or locality basis.) Within universities it is rather unusual for leadership favouring W/P to be strong and explicit, given other, competing and more prestigious, policy pulls alongside financial stringency. Moreover, academic staff generally feel themselves to be excluded from the table where policy is made. Since they are not effectively involved or even consulted in the university's W/P policy-making, they then tend not to get personally committed. Even where there is top-level commitment, W/P energy then leaches away below faculty levels in and below departments, in the places where behaviour determines its success or failure.

On a different plane, it was felt that there was a paucity of influential champions of W/P; that diversity, for all the official rhetoric celebrating and promoting it, was still dishonoured by hierarchy and by powerful, widely held, considerations of status. This problem is exacerbated by the competitive marketisation of HE, such that reputation has high monetary value in terms of student recruitment. It calls for stronger national leadership and financial leverage than our traditions of institutional autonomy allow for us politically to fully honour – and financially support – diversity over hierarchy. We tend to talk diversity but fund sameness.

Although we do well in terms of retention, that is to say system efficiency narrowly defined, there has been no paradigm shift from the time-honoured full-time pre-experience 'front-loading' model of (initial) higher education; this despite the reality of high numbers of part-time students, and the outstanding example of the Open University. We have yet to achieve 'mode-free' status, whereby students move through the institution (or indeed across institutions) taking variable periods of time to complete a programme and qualification, their 'status' as full- or part-time invisible and generally unknown, as well as formally irrelevant, to the lecturer. (There is of course 'tutorial' relevance in terms of time available for study, and competition for time from other life roles, but this now applies to most 'full-time' students as well, even prior to the introduction of top-up fees and a higher debt regime.)

On a broader plane, it was felt that the system and its institutions were still essentially centred on the institution- (or supply-side) rather than the student. As noted above there has been no attempt to lower, much less dissolve, sector boundaries with FE. Some indeed perceive the re-creation of an older binary divide within HE, and the FE sector continues to suffer a lack of political confidence in it and therefore of self-confidence as well. Finally, less irrelevant than it may appear, there is a failure of the system to support public intellectuals. These appear to have evacuated the public domain, leaving the sector more vulnerable to charges of irrelevance, and feeding old stereotypes which keep academic sheep away from vocational goats.

A distinction may be made between missed opportunities and those that appear stalled or precarious. On the broader plane there is regional devolution and policy-making. This appears to be at least stalled following the hostile regional assembly referendum in the North-East, and despite – or possibly even because of? – the evident success of devolution, especially in Scotland but perhaps also in Wales.

Research competitiveness played out through the research assessment exercise (RAE) is –albeit unintendedly – the enemy of both W/P and regional engagement. The idea of Mode Two knowledge production widens the understanding of research, but there has been only modest progress here in the decade since the term and concept were popularised, certainly not enough to offset the heavy weight of the RAE favouring a more familiar research paradigm that pulls away from W/P embedded within regional engagement.

It is too soon to refer to Lifelong Learning Networks (LLNs) as stalled, much less failed. Indeed, these show promise of cutting through failures of regionality and of partnership, within and beyond an HE/FE 'system' – especially as their formal remit to address 14-19 vocational access shows promise of widening out to a broader approach to mostly regional and locality-based partnership for access and participation. While caution remains, LLNs moved quickly beyond the outright hostility that greeted them in the early months to something like guarded optimism, and even enthusiasm to join in make a go of them.

It would have passed without question to call foundation degrees both problematic and stalled a short while ago. They were plagued by questions about simply re-badging earlier (HNC and HND) vocational qualifications, about (lack of) demand and lack of (private sector) employer support – an unwanted sub-degree that did not lead into either good employment or completed (conventional) higher education. With new funded additional students numbers (ASNs) coming the FD way, and prestigious universities joining in selectively, what did indeed appear to have stalled is now moving forward more confidently. Associated with better valuing of the vocational, with the emerging LLNs, and with a political determination to put new funds into FDs despite the middle class market preference for familiar honours degrees, FDs might come to represent a breakthrough favouring W/P, even though they may not be seen as a pure W/P access initiative.

Aimhigher itself appears to be making progress, albeit within a moderate agenda that could end up being more about securing supply chains than with seriously *widening* participation. None the less, if school compacting becomes well bedded down and normalised, it may have the effect of normalising the idea of going to university, and eroding the notion that 'university's only for other people, not for people like me'.

Less amenable still to cultural change may be the attitude of staff within universities who feel overburdened and undervalued. For these, unless they have a personal passion for equity, W/P that brings in more diverse and less well prepared students simply means more difficult working conditions, more risk of punishment if withdrawal rates rise, less time for research. The well-founded notion that 'what is better for access is better for all' may have a long way to run before it wins the majority of staff.

Let us end with a quick word about pitfalls and word traps. Prominent among these is *quality*. Fear of audits, fear of 'wastage' or failed students, discourages all but the most determined institutional heads and the most passionate teachers, breeding *risk averseness*. *Compacts* can be effective in raising aspirations even in 'failing schools' and sink neighbourhoods; but they can, while masquerading as W/P, also be about no more than supply-chain 'cherry-picking'.

There are some warm and fuzzy terms such as *access movement* and *access community* that tempt people into a ghetto; here a few people appointed to express the university's W/P policies and nominal access mission are marginalised from the sites both of power and of policy-in-action. They are able to do very little. Then there is the temptation to emphasise high quality (even *world class*) and conclude that being smaller is better. *System contraction* will almost certainly prevent and reverse W/P.

Diversity is something of a weasel word, as we have already seen. And there is the national preference for fixing on *the individual* at the cost of considering the group – very evident when one looks by contrast at universities in 'social Europe'. We prefer *catchments* to *places* in recruiting and securing supply. The *private sector* enjoys politically correct preference over the public – although it is mainly the latter that supports foundation degrees. Of course *vocational* continues to be grossly abused in its meaning, as well as carrying an apparently indelible stain of inferiority from which doctors and lawyers remain exempt. Not to extend this discussion, we should also reflect in this context and in this way on the use and connotations of *full-time*, of *the student experience*, of *personalisation, self-directed*, and *individualisation*, as well as of *flexibility*.

Despite recognising the pitfalls and gentle self-delusions that not only politicians employ in playing these word games, the symposium was not despondent. Perhaps it was the effect of meeting sharply critical but still unwavering champions and scholars of W/P from across all parts of the system that left an upbeat sense. Many road blocks to widening participation are hard to remove, some even hard to see, so deeply cultural are they, so embedded and ingrained.

The capacity of an institutional culture to go on reproducing itself as its people come go and new ones come is awesome. Nevertheless, the symposium noted in conclusion that there will be a massive turnover of staff in the next few years as the baby boom generation retires. Most of those working in universities will not then talk about and yearn for the good old days, because they were not there and did not experience them. Maybe we should not count on it, but is it possible that before too long the good old boys and the good old days will be for ever gone?

Contributors

Liz Allen is National Official Higher Education, NATFHE – The University and College Lecturers' Union. Liz Allen has national responsibility for Higher Education Policy at NATFHE. Current areas of work include widening participation, the research-teaching relationship, support for part time lecturers, and e-learning. She is the author of the research 'In From the Cold – Part-time teaching and professional development' (2001), and of policy publications on a range of issues including the pedagogical implications of e-learning, peer observation of teaching and strategies for rewarding teaching. Committee memberships have included the government's HE Research Forum (2004) and membership of the Council of the Institute for Learning and Teaching in HE (ILTHE)

She is also a member of the Central Arbitration Committee. She has held an honorary research fellowship at the University of Bradford (2002–05) and will be awarded an honorary fellowship from York St John College in November 2005.

Chris Duke is Associate Director for Adult Learning with Action on Access and for Higher Education with NIACE. He is also Professor of Regional Partnerships and Learning at RMIT University in Melbourne and an honorary professor at the universities of Leicester and Stirling. He has worked at the universities of Greenwich, Leeds and Warwick, Auckland, UWS Nepean and the Australian National University, and has published widely on higher and adult education and lifelong learning, especially on policy, engagement and development, access and equity issues, and on organisation behaviour and change.

R.H. Fryer CBE is National Director for Widening Participation in Learning, Department of Health. In that role Bob has responsibility for devising, leading and supporting the implementation of a strategy to open up access to learning and employment in NHS professions, to widen participation in learning for NHS staff who are currently excluded from learning and to stimulate learning for all across the NHS.

Prior to taking up his current post on secondment, Bob Fryer was the founding Chief Executive of NHSU from February 2002 to February 2005.

Bob is currently a Director of Investors in People UK and Chair of the Learning and Skills Council's Distributed and Electronic Learning Group. He is also Chair of the Defence Education and Skills Advisory Board.

Geoff Layer is Pro-Vice Chancellor (Learning and Teaching) at the University of Bradford and Professor of Lifelong Learning. He is also the Director of Action on Access, the National Co-ordination team for widening participation in higher education in England. He was the founding Dean of the School of Lifelong Education and Development at Bradford and prior to that Head of Access and Guidance at Sheffield Hallam University.

Derek Longhurst is Director of Foundation Degree Forward. He has worked at the Universities of Greenwich, Sunderland, Minnesota and Staffordshire where he was a Dean of School of Arts, Humanities and Social Sciences for a decade. His teaching and research background is in the field of cultural and media policy.

He is currently involved in QCA consultations about the development of 14–19 specialised Diplomas and the 'Framework for Achievement'.

Ceri Nursaw is Head of the City and Regional Office at the University of Leeds and has responsibility for widening participation, community relations and partnership development. She is Director of the National Compact Scheme and was recently appointed as a lead consultant for Action on Access.

Her work has predominately been within higher education although she has held posts in a local authority and Government Office.

She has an MBA and MSc from the University of Leeds.

Stephen Sheedy was born, brought up and schooled in Liverpool. After graduating in English from the University of Oxford, Stephen went into teaching and has worked in grammar schools, comprehensive schools, colleges of further education and sixth form colleges. He has been Principal of Queen Mary's College in Basingstoke for the past ten years and is a member of the Executive Group of the Secondary Heads Association, which he represents on the National Partnership Board for Aimhigher.

Mary Stuart is Pro Vice Chancellor at the University of Sussex. She is also Associate Director Research and Curriculum for Action on Access. She has worked in further and higher education for eighteen years. She has published extensively in the field of widening participation in higher education.

Liz Thomas is Senior Adviser for Widening Participation at the Higher Education Academy. Liz is actively involved in research, policy and practice related to widening participation and improving students' learning experiences. She is particularly interested in the retention and success of students from under-represented groups, and institutional change to support this. She has managed and participated in national and international research projects on these and related issues. Recent studies include a HEFCE-funded review of widening participation research literature, a national study of widening participation practice, funded by Universities UK and the Standing Conference of Principals and an international, qualitative study about young, working class students who leave higher education early, funded by the Joseph Rowntree Foundation. In addition to research reports and journal articles, Liz has written and edited five books on access and widening participation and is co-editor of the peer-reviewed journal *Widening Participation and Lifelong Learning*.

David Watson is an historian and Professor of Higher Education Management at the Institute of Education, University of London. He was Vice-Chancellor of the University of Brighton (formerly Brighton Polytechnic) between 1990 and 2005.

His academic interests are in the history of American ideas and in higher education policy. His most recent books are *Lifelong Learning and the University* (1998), *Managing Strategy* (2000), *New Directions in Professional Higher Education* (2000), *Higher Education and the Lifecourse* (2003), and *Managing Institutional Self-Study* (2005).

He was the elected chair of the Universities Association for Continuing Education between 1994 and 1998, and chaired the Longer Term Strategy Group of Universities UK between 1999 and 2005. He is a Trustee of the Nuffield Foundation and a Companion of the Institute of Management. He was knighted in 1998 for services to higher education.

Kevin Whitston joined the Higher Education Funding Council as Head of Widening Participation at the end of 2003. He was formerly Director of the Widening Participation Unit at the University of Birmingham and prior to that taught for many years in trade union education.

John Widdowson is Principal and Chief Executive, New College Durham. John Widdowson joined New College Durham as Principal and Chief Executive in August 1998. John began his career as a lawyer in local government after which he held a series of teaching posts in Derbyshire and East Anglia. Before joining New College, he was Vice Principal at Cambridge Regional College for ten years.

New College is a Mixed Economy College and as such is a significant provider of full-time and part-time vocational higher education in the county and in the region.

He is Chair of the Further Education National Consortium and the Mixed Economy Group of Colleges. He is also Chair of Aimhigher County Durham.

Dianne Willcocks is Principal at York St John College. An advocate and practitioner for socially inclusive HE, Professor Willcocks' major commitment is to promote higher education that engages with the needs of modern communities for social, cultural and economic well-being. She was previously Assistant Principal at Sheffield Hallam University and Director of Research at the University of North London. She engages and publishes in the contemporary debate around new learners and new learning styles in higher education.

She is a governor/trustee of the Aimhigher National Partnership Board; the Board of Higher York; and serves on the York Diocesan Board of Education. She is Chair of the Standing Conference of Principals and a member for HEFCE on the Widening Participation Strategy Committee, and the Teaching (T) Funding Sounding Board. She is a member of CIHE, the Council for Industry and Higher Education. Recently serving on the Yorkshire Arts Board for 6 years, Professor Willcocks is currently on the Board of Yorkshire Film Archive; the York Leisure Partnership; and the York Museums Trust. She Chairs the York Theatre Royal Trust.

Index